WORKING WITH JUNIORS AT CHURCH

Working With Juniors at Church

DOROTHY LaCROIX HILL

HENRY M. BULLOCK, *General Editor*

A B I N G D O N   P R E S S

NEW YORK • NASHVILLE

WORKING WITH JUNIORS AT CHURCH

Copyright MCMLV by Pierce & Washabaugh

Library of Congress Catalog Card Number: 55-6764

Scripture quotations, unless otherwise noted, are from the Revised Standard Version of the Bible and are copyright 1946,
1952 by Division of Christian Education of the National Council of the Churches of Christ in the United States of America.

SET UP, PRINTED, AND BOUND BY THE
PARTHENON PRESS, AT NASHVILLE,
TENNESSEE, UNITED STATES OF AMERICA

BV
1546
H551 w

Contents

Contents

Let Us Be Joyful

"Come, let us be joyful"
As we teach our children!
For they are made of the stuff
Which God has made
To be His highest creation.
They are made of the stuff
Of which God is a part. . . .
And He is a part of them.

For no gold mine ever held
Such possibilities, nor the
Bottom of the ocean with its
Unfathomable treasures,
Nor the mass of stone in which Michelangelo
Visioned loveliness.
A child holds secret surprise and delight
For those who want to teach him.

"Come, let us be joyful"
As we teach our children!
For if we teach them well,
We will have *cause* for great rejoicing.
Not that they will remember us,
But that they may live more abundantly,
And in so living, *become the leaders*
For which the world cries out.[1]

[1] From *Stories About Jesus* by Mary Cureton Brumley. Copyright 1950 by Pierce and Smith. By permission of Abingdon Press.

CHAPTER ONE

A Look at Learning

IT IS SUNDAY MORNING, and our juniors are coming to church. Their teachers are arriving, too. We may be quite certain that these serious-minded, mature adults are intent upon teaching something to their classes. Perhaps it is an important "truth" taken from their teachers' texts, a Bible story which they plan to have the juniors read from their study books, or a verse or two from the Bible itself. The junior superintendent has in mind a story to tell, hymns to be announced, a passage of Scripture to read, the thoughts to be expressed in a prayer. Most of these persons are thinking chiefly about what *they* will say and what *they* will do as they teach.

But why are the juniors coming? Some are here because to their families the church is important. Their fathers and mothers have come with them. These fathers and mothers are interested in and concerned with the teaching program of the church. Many juniors attend because they meet their friends at church. This is an age when friends are important. Other fortunate children make their way to church week after week because they find interesting work and study there, as well as fellowship.

Many others come because their parents feel that the church is a good place for children to be, although the parents themselves may not attend. These parents hope vaguely that the young son or daughter of the family will learn something good. Few could put into words just what they would like that good learning to be. Usually parents are pleased if a Bible story has been included in the session. They may ask at the dinner table what Bill or Susan has learned at church. They are likely to be baffled or mildly amused when Bill or Susan answers, "Nothing!"

Granted that juniors find a peculiar pleasure in baffling and amusing adults, still most of the boys and girls honestly do not think that they have "learned" anything. Probably they, their parents, and all too many teachers would say that learning is being able to repeat what one has heard.

Repeating what one has heard, upon request, is usually difficult and often dull. On rare occasions a speaker has shared with us something so thrilling and so challenging that we find ourselves telling it even to those who have not asked to hear. Yet we know that much has been lost in the retelling. Invariably we close by saying feebly and with futility, "I wish you could have been there!"

In so doing, we are proving that we know much more about learning than we think we know. We are saying, in effect, "Something happened to me there. To fully understand, you would have had to share that experience." Or we may be saying that something we have always thought true has now, because of this experience, become a conviction for us. We feel impelled to share it or to take a stand for or against it. We are saying that we have learned.

What Did You Do?

If at the Sunday dinner table instead of, "What did you learn?" father would ask, "What happened today at church? What did you do?" his junior might reply with a torrent of words. For wherever juniors meet, a great deal is happening. The junior who pours out all that "happened," all that he "did," is actually telling us what he learned, if we are able to interpret.

"What did you do at church today?"

"We just sat, and Mrs. —— read out of the quarterly." ("We learned that the church is a place of boredom and inactivity, where people just sit and listen to other people talk or read.")

10

"What happened at church today?"

"We finished reading the story of Joseph the way it is in the Bible, you know. We can read our new Bibles (Revised Standard Version), but Mrs. —— makes stories sound so exciting that we asked her to read most of it. Then we counted off and made committees of five. Each committee dramatized one part of the story, not saying anything, you know. The others guessed what was being acted out. Our committee showed Joseph's servants finding his cup in Benjamin's sack. I could read that to you. It's toward the end of Genesis."

("We learned that the Bible has stories we can enjoy. We are learning to read it and to find our favorite stories and passages in it.")

"What happened at church today?"

"We fellows really had fun! We got the girls crazy, and Miss ——, too. She couldn't do a thing!"

("We learned that the church is a place where one can act like a rowdy. It is not a place where boys and girls work and learn.")

Yes, even when the junior thinks he has learned nothing at church, he has learned much. It may not be what the teacher thinks he has learned. It may not be what he was expected to learn, but he has learned, for all of us are learning all the time. We are learning many different things at once, ways of thinking, feeling, acting. Learning begins in infancy and goes on to our dying day. It is made up of change. We are constantly rubbing up against experiences which force us to change—other people, new ideas, difficult problems and situations, decisions which have to be made, forces of nature. We find ourselves thinking differently, feeling differently, responding in new ways to situations, to what happens, to what people ask of us, to God, and to his will for us.

Some learning helps growth because the person is changing in desirable ways. Some learning interferes with wholesome growth when the learner accepts an untrue or mistaken belief, or becomes the victim of misguided emotions. His response to persons, to situations, to God, can be no better than his thinking and feeling.

A book-loving junior was asked if he were a ballplayer. "No," he said carefully, "but I am learning."

Both he and his parents had recognized that he was losing out on wholesome fellowship with his own age group because most of the boys in the neighborhood played ball all their waking hours.

"I'm just not good at it," Bill said defensively.

"That's all right, Bill," his father replied. "The fellows who are better at it get to play the most. But any chap can know enough about ball to fill in when a team needs an extra player. A good mitt would help you."

The new mitt did help. So did the evening games in the back yard—all "just for fun"—with the whole family, younger neighbors, and gradually other boys Bill's age all taking a turn at bat and in the field.

Bill found himself learning many things at one time. He was growing not only in skill, but in wholesome feelings toward the game, toward the fellows who played it all the time, and best of all, toward himself.

Bill discovered that learning is changing. He saw himself little by little changing to a fellow who no longer drew back his hand rather than take the sting of a hard-thrown ball, who accepted the offer of a post in left field instead of shaking his head, who felt comfortable on the bench. His parents knew that learning was all these things, and a little more.

It was Bill sounding different and a changed boy when someone asked, "What do the kids in your neighborhood do, Bill?"

"Oh, they mostly play ball," but without any bitterness in the words.

12

"Are you a ball player, Bill?"

"No, but I'm learning," with cheerfulness and a touch of assurance.

The day might never come when Bill could answer, "Yes." He could say that he had learned only when his catching and hitting, running and throwing, would almost always count toward victory for his team. But in the meantime he was *learning.*

Learning—Good or Bad?

Wayne was learning, too. His learning was taking place at church, but it was not good.

When he participated in a laboratory class with boys and girls from several churches, an adult leader said to the instructor, "See if you can find out what is wrong with Wayne. His teacher has so much trouble with him. She says he is mean. She likes children and knows how to work with them, too."

Wayne and his pal were handsome, lively nine-year-olds. The instructor from the first moment kept them too busy for mischief. She liked them, and they liked her. But in the second session something went wrong. Each child had been given a copy of the Revised Standard Version of the Bible, and the class set to work to make some important discoveries about the New Testament. Wayne snatched the Bible from the girl who was passing them. Rapidly he began to thumb through the pages, paying little attention to the teacher's simple directions for finding books, chapters, and verses. Presently he slammed his Bible shut and sat back with folded arms, sullenness settled like a cloud over his bright face. The instructor did not understand what had happened. She said nothing.

The next day the boys and girls found six large teaching pictures in the room, six Bible references on the blackboard. Copies of the Bible, paper, and pencils were ready for use. The juniors were asked to study each picture, copy the titles on a sheet of paper, read the references silently, and write opposite each picture title the name of the Gospel in which they had discovered that story.

Wayne enjoyed looking at the pictures. But once again when he took the Bible, his actions became strange, "frenzied" was the word in the mind of the watching teacher. She sat down beside him and repeated step by step the directions for finding the Gospels. But as she tried to help him, Wayne's attention darted from one child to another. He tried to read the first reference, but his eyes left the page with every few words.

"Read it to me," the teacher invited.

Wayne read well, so that was not the problem. When the first child announced that he had finished, Wayne's face twisted with anger. He slammed his Bible shut and walked to a far chair, his arms folded and his expression sullen. He took no more interest in the session. The Bible seemed to be at the heart of the difficulty. Finally the instructor inquired how the Bible was used with juniors in Wayne's church. Each Sunday when the department met together, a Bible drill was held. Seventy or more children competed to see who could find each reference first and read aloud just enough to show that the right verse had been found. Members of the fourth grade were seldom first, but apparently Wayne could not accept defeat, even by older and more experienced children. His father was a university professor. A good deal was expected of him in the way of scholastic achievement, yet the Bible defeated him Sunday after Sunday. In his passionate efforts to be first he was missing out on the basic learnings which could have helped him become more skillful in handling the Bible. Already the very sight of a Bible was associated in his mind with failure. His emotions began to seethe as soon as copies were distributed. So strong had the pattern of failure become that in this new situation where the Bible was used as a source of needed information, not in meaningless competition, Wayne could not recognize the difference.

Wayne had accepted a wrong idea about the Bible. He thought of it as an instrument of competition. His efforts to use it in this way had created most unwholesome feelings. As a result his response to the Bible, and indeed to the whole of his church-school experience, could not be anything else but disagreeable, both to himself and to his teacher.

Vernon was learning, too. Like Wayne he was learning at church school, and his learning had to do with the Bible. "What did you do today?" asked his mother.

Vernon's eyes lit up with enthusiasm. The fourth-grade class had started work on a choral reading, Psalms 150, to be shared with the adult classes three Sundays hence.

"It's about musical instruments, you know," Vernon explained. "The girls are the 'strings and pipe,' and we are the cymbals—'praise him with loud clashing cymbals!' it says."

"You know some of it, don't you?" his mother asked.

"Oh, no!" said Vernon. "We didn't learn it; we just read it."

"How does it begin?" asked his older brother.

"Why"— Vernon pondered a moment, then phrase by phrase, line by line, to his own astonishment he repeated the entire passage. He jumped from his chair in great excitement and ran to get his Bible, "to be sure I got it right." He had it right. He turned to Psalms 95 and read the lines which his class had studied. His mother reminded him that he knew Psalms 100, and he read this with pleasure. His father asked him to read Psalms 23.

Then an idea came to life in Vernon's quick mind. "Say," he said, "whenever we are supposed to read in Psalms for family worship, may I read?"

Vernon's experience with the Bible was helping him to grow

15

in the very ways which his teacher, his church, and his parents desired. It was leading him to want to keep on learning from and using his Bible. It is important to note that when the church learning was lifted up, understood, and appreciated *at home,* Vernon moved forward into a still finer response to the Bible, one which under the guidance and encouragement of his parents might become permanent.

Donnie was a question asker. His class was discovering how early Old Testament leaders grew in their knowledge of God. Donnie was greatly puzzled by the many records of times when God spoke to these long-ago men.

"Could they hear him?" he asked. "Does he say real words now? He would have to know all kinds of languages, wouldn't he? Did he ever say anything to you?"

The teacher said that she had never heard God speak actual words. However, she was perfectly sure that at times he had told her something that helped her very much.

"What did he tell you?" Donnie asked eagerly.

"Well," she said, "each time I was very much troubled about some family problem. I kept worrying about what I would do if things turned out the way that I hoped they wouldn't. And each time, at a moment when I was trying to rest, when I was very quiet, and all alone, I knew that whatever happened, everything would be all right. God told me not to worry any more, and I didn't."

Donnie was still puzzled about how you could hear God without hearing words.

His teacher turned for help to their minister. He was greatly interested and deeply concerned that Donnie and the other juniors should grow in their understanding of God through this experience. He spent a half-hour with the junior department the next Sunday.

This was his message, although not in these exact words:

"Some of the most puzzling things in the world are quite easy to understand when we make the wonderful discovery that our bodies are not us. They are only houses in which the real you and the real I live for a while. The real you and the real I are like God. So that is the part of us that he speaks to, and he does not need to use words. He loves us so much and understands us so well that he knows what we are thinking. He knows the kind of persons we are and want to be, even when we are not acting our best. He knows when things trouble us, and he is always trying to help us. If we were better listeners, we would hear him speaking to us more often. Probably we will never hear words. We will just know that he is there and that he is helping us. When that happens to you, it will be so real and so sure that in telling someone about it you may use words, as Joshua did. He heard God say, 'Be strong and of good courage; be not frightened, neither be dismayed; for the Lord your God is with you wherever you go.' "

The minister added that God speaks to us constantly in many other ways, through his provision of parents to love and care for us, through the beauty of our earth home, through planning a world with all that we need in it, through the Bible, through friends and teachers. All of these say daily and hourly that God loves us and cares about us.

With reverence and gladness the boys and girls sang a song they had known for a long time, but never before thought much about:

> "God speaks to us . . .
> A melody of love." [1]

Teachers felt the unity of the group as the minister voiced a prayer that each one might learn to listen, not with his ears, but with his real self; that each might often know surely when God was making him strong, helping to direct him into right choices, and rejoicing with him in all the good and happy experiences of his life.

[1] From *Hymns for Junior Worship* (Westminster Press).

Something very good for their Christian growing happened that day to those boys and girls. They grew in the consciousness of God's constant presence. They began to understand a bit more clearly what God is like and how he guides and helps his children. Perhaps best of all, they felt trust and confidence, the foundation for coming experiences of listening for God's guidance and encouragement. Some understood more fully than others. But all were at least a little changed in their understanding of God and of themselves, a little changed in their feeling about him, a little more ready to give heed to God the father.

Ours is the opportunity to guide boys and girls in discovering what God wants them to do and to be. Ours is the privilege of awakening their admiration for Jesus, the Son of God; of leading them to desire to pattern their lives after his. This is the kind of learning we want for them.

Then let us take to this task our solid, true, everyday understanding that learning means changing, learning means growing. Let us believe with surety and conviction that the ways in which all of us learn are inborn, a part of God's creation. When we understand the pattern of learning, when we use it with skill and with love to help boys and girls live increasingly God-conscious, God-directed lives, then we are giving back to the Creator some small part of his best gift to mankind.

Yes, Bill and Mary learn at church in just the same ways that they learn at home and at school. The process is the same whether they are discovering how to build a birdhouse, prepare a meal, or do a creditable job of cleaning their rooms. It is the same whether they are finding out the role of corn or cotton in the nation's economy or making discoveries about the nature and the will of God.

First, someone or something must help them want to learn. Then there is much for them to find out, and this is something they need to do for themselves in so far as possible. Next they must have opportunities to put their discoveries to use in ways which seem worth while to them. The whole experience must be strongly flavored with good feelings, with satisfaction in the results, so that boys and girls will wish to use their new learnings again and again until they become natural, usual ways of responding.

CHAPTER TWO

Linking Teaching to Learning

ALTHOUGH WE MAY have differing ideas about how to teach, all of us must agree that the purpose of teaching is to help persons learn. Therefore a teacher's first need in order to work successfully with a class of boys and girls is to discover what learning is and how it takes place. We have discovered that what happens to persons causes them to change in ways of thinking, of feeling, and of responding. They learn from their experiences.

Four questions about how to teach are commonly asked by those who are trying to work with children in the church:

"How shall I present the lesson?"

"How can I make the children listen?"

"How can I put the thought over?"

"How can I make the lesson stick?"

These questions suggest an entirely different concept of learning. They would make it seem (1) that learning is passively accepting truths offered by the teacher; (2) that if boys and girls sit quietly and listen, they will learn; (3) that there must be some magic way of "telling" which will transfer the idea or thought of the lesson from the teacher's mind to that of the child; and (4) that after the "lesson has been taught," something additional must be said or done to "apply" it to the child's life. These ideas about learning are no more true in the field of religion than they are in everyday life.

We cannot imagine a father saying to the young son who wishes to make a birdhouse, "Now just memorize the measurements and blueprints, Son. When you can sketch them perfectly, you will know how to make a birdhouse." We know

20

well that this ten-year-old must have the firsthand experience of making the birdhouse and many other articles of wood. We know that, if his early experiences with carpentry are satisfying, he will continue to build and to take pride and find pleasure in his growing skill.

Every parent watches with trepidation as his boy or girl sets forth on that first bicycle. How many times he has "told" this child the rules for riding safely! How many times he has called attention to mistakes made by other bicyclists! How desperately he wishes that there were some magic way to make his child "apply" the rules from his first moment on a bicycle! The rules have been heard, and the child can repeat them. In this sense he knows them. He recognizes their importance and intends to obey them when he begins to ride. These are important first steps in learning. Yet the rules will be really learned only as the young rider makes his own decisions about when to signal, when to turn, when to use his brakes. He will really learn only when he is turned free with his bicycle to learn by doing.

If we learn through our experiences, lessons should consist primarily of experiences; and teaching should be largely the guiding of experiences.

What Is an Experience?

If teachers of religion must plan and guide experiences, we need to understand what an experience is for a group and for individual boys and girls. We must discover ways to help good things happen which will accomplish with children the purposes we have for their growing in the Christian faith. We must be ready to help them do the things through which they learn.

Although it may seem difficult to define, all of us know what an experience is. When we say, "Now that was an experience!" we are invariably describing something which has happened to us.

Our friends reply, "That must have been an experience!"

They, too, know what the first important element in any experience is—it must happen to you.

The second important element in an experience is that because this has happened to you, you are a little different. You think a little differently. You feel a little differently. You will respond a little differently to a similar happening in the future. If the experience has been extremely vivid, one of those unforgettable moments, you may change greatly in a very short period of time. If you find yourself caught up in an ongoing series of happenings, all related to the same kind of situation, you may change more slowly, but just as surely. If the experience is fleeting, not very intense, the change may be slight; but there will be a change, nevertheless. Some change will be good. Some change will be bad. Whether the change is good or bad may be determined by a guiding person who shares in the experience.

Some children are extremely sensitive and timid. All their experiences will either help or hinder them in growing toward happy, confident living. The parent who is annoyed that his child is "different" will hinder development. The helpful one will accept him as a person who is a bit slower than some in his emotional growing. Such a parent will help the child find courage to play in a neighbor's yard, to go alone to a playmate's party, to master skills which foster both self-respect and the respect of others. Learning to read, to jump rope, to swim, to play the piano, may unlock a new world of freedom and of satisfying experiences with other children. The older boy or girl may be greatly helped by an adult who firmly but kindly insists that he conquer unreasoning fear of taking a message to a person he has never met or telephoning to find out the hour that a movie will begin. Triumph over difficulties like these will encourage him to undertake harder experiences, to "do it anyway, even if you are afraid."

If he discovers that attending a party, or giving one, "is not so bad after all," he will be growing toward social

22

competence. He will be fortunate if he has a sympathetic, understanding, well-balanced adult to help him look objectively, and sometimes humorously, at his triumphs and failures in winning and keeping friends, in making a place for himself in school and play groups.

The teacher who looks for the timid child's strong points and abilities, who helps him use them to win deserved recognition among his fellows, is fostering his growth. His development is hindered by the teacher who ridicules his backwardness or is "glad that at least one child is no trouble." Such an experience may turn him still farther back into loneliness and unsocial living.

Through all that happens to him every day this child will be changing. The way that he reacts to experiences with adults, and especially to experiences with his own age group, will determine the direction of his growing.

Many years ago a young junior was shopping with her mother in a large city. As they stood waiting to cross the street, a large van drawn by two teams of horses came swiftly through the intersection. Right before the child's eyes a little old lady stepped into the street and was trampled.

The little girl began to scream hysterically, "Take me away! Take me home!"

The wise mother led her back from the street and, planting her firmly against the large window of a department store, gave her a vigorous shake, saying kindly but urgently, "Listen to me! Do you hear? We are going home because there is nothing we can do to help. The police have come. They have called an ambulance. They know how to help better than we do. But if there was even one little thing we could do to help that hurt lady, we would stay right here and do it. Do you understand?"

Even in her hysteria the little girl heard. She understood. Always afterward that scene came to mind when emergencies had to be met. She did not run away. She stayed to do whatever could be done. She responded differently than in that first experience. She was different. She had learned. Her mother had guided the learning in the right direction. It could just as easily have been the opposite kind of learning, and the child's impulse to run from unpleasant scenes could have been strengthened instead of uprooted. Her mother had played the role of a wise teacher.

This was one of the extremely vivid kinds of experience. For the brief span of its duration neither mother nor child thought of anything else. Both were feeling deeply about what had happened. Both did something because of what had happened, but each did something different. The child reacted to fright and shock by screaming, by trying to run away. The mother doubtless reacted, but she also acted purposefully because she had learned well in similar experiences. Her own fright and shock, as real as the child's, were put aside in concern for the woman who was hurt, in concern for the child who might have been seriously injured in her growing.

In defining an experience, then, we may say that it is always something which happens to you causing you to change to some degree. You change because your interest, your emotions, and your energies are all actively engaged by what is happening. You think, you feel, you act or react, and as you do so, a pattern of thinking, feeling, and acting is set up for similar happenings in the future. The pattern may grow stronger and stronger if experiences cause it to be repeated again and again. It may fade away if nothing happens or nothing is done to strengthen it. It is even possible that this pattern may be broken down and another pattern established.

Planned Experiences

In the Sunday-morning sessions, in vacation school, in additional sessions, in all the learning situations which make up the church school, our children participate in quiet, ongoing kinds of experience. Some are those suggested and developed within our lesson materials. Others come from the purposes the group sets up, the plans which the boys and girls and their teachers make together. Still others grow out of special needs of the class or of individual members. Successful teachers, as they study the lesson materials, begin to plan experiences which will lead to important discoveries, new ways of thinking, the kinds of attitudes and responses which represent Christian growth for their boys and girls.

Just as truly as in the vivid, highly emotional experience of the little girl witnessing an accident, so in church-school learnings the interest, feelings and energies of the pupils must be actively engaged. If they are not, if the junior is not interested, if his feelings are those of boredom, indifference, or active dislike for what goes on in his class, then his responses will all be in the direction of disrupting behavior, of irregular attendance, and perhaps of disdain, indifference to, or ridicule of religious experience. He will be learning because each of us is learning all the time, since we cannot help but respond in one way or another to what is happening to us; but his learning may not be good.

For You to Do

Read the following story of Mike and his fifth-grade church-school class. Make a list of all the experiences in which the boys and girls participated.

Which were probably suggested in the lesson materials?

Which grew out of the pupils' purposes and interests?

Which experience was unplanned, but very important?

Learning at Church and at Home

Among the ten-year-olds enrolled in one church, Mike was probably the liveliest and the most talkative. He was also one of the most regular in attendance. During the fall months this fifth-grade class studied a unit from their denominational course of study called "The Homeland of Jesus." In early sessions of the unit they engaged in activities planned to help them grow in a sense of the reality of the Bible land and therefore of the Bible itself.

Material from their pupils' books, View-master reels picturing Palestine, and stereoscope pictures helped them to "view all the land," as Abraham and Lot had done long before. They were astonished to discover that it is actually possible to see snow-capped Mt. Hermon to the north and the Dead Sea to the south, to glimpse the waters of the Mediterranean and the high plateaus beyond the Jordan. To carry home to parents their discovery about the small size of Palestine, each junior made a construction-paper pattern of the map of that country, cut to the same scale as road maps of their own state. At home they were able to place this pattern upon a road map, thus showing their families that the distance between Jerusalem and Bethlehem is no greater than an after-dinner drive, that the 150-mile length of Palestine is less than that of most states in the United States.

Recalling a Psalm studied in fourth grade, they pictured the poet upon some mountaintop exclaiming:

> In his hand are the depths of the earth;
>   the heights of the mountains are his also.
> The sea is his, for he made it;
>   for his hands formed the dry land.
>
> O come, let us worship and bow down,
>   let us kneel before the LORD, our Maker!

With night scenes of Palestine before them, taken from the teaching pictures provided by their denomination, they imagined the feelings of the long-ago poet who wrote:

> Before the mountains were brought forth,
>   or ever thou hadst formed the earth and the world,
>   from everlasting to everlasting thou art God.

26

For a thousand years in thy sight
are but as yesterday when it is past,
or as a watch in the night.

The land of Palestine began to mean to thoughtful boys and girls a place which stirred in its people deep, wonderful, and true thoughts of God. This set the group to finding out about some of the ways in which these Bible people worshiped God.

Pupils, parents, and teachers planned together to visit the Jewish temple in their city on the evening when Jewish worshipers were celebrating the Feast of Booths. In preparation the group discovered in the Bible the ancient laws for keeping this festival of thanksgiving at the close of Palestine's important fruit harvest. So that the service would have meaning for the group, they examined the prayer book of the temple and learned to recite in Hebrew the "Shema," which one rabbi described as the "Jew's pledge of loyalty": "Hear, O Israel: The Lord our God, the Lord is one." From a copy of the temple hymnal they learned to sing a song of the festival which the rabbi planned to use in the service. In their pupils' books they read a description of what the service would be like and of articles which they would see in the temple, both because this was a Jewish place of worship and because it was the season of Sukkoth, or the Feast of Booths.

After their visit to the temple the boys and girls began to make plans for sharing with families and friends what they were learning about the homeland of Jesus and its people's ways of worshiping God. They chose to work out the two-scene dramatization of the Feast of Booths given in their pupils' books. The first scene pictured the festival being kept as it originally was in Palestine—a harvest thanksgiving time when gifts of the crops were carried up to the Temple, and the people lived for eight days in simple shelters like those set up for watching over their harvest fields. The second

27

scene showed a Jewish family in America remembering this thanksgiving time with a brief period of worship at their dinner table.

The play was given on a Sunday evening before a potluck supper for all families of the fifth grade. Songs and Scripture which had been learned were also shared. Filmstrips of what is taking place today in the new land of Israel were shown. The boys and girls told about their plan for showing their interest in Palestine and their concern for its people. They had chosen to make a gift of trees for the Children's Memorial Forest on the eroded hillsides near Nazareth.

Mike was tremendously interested in this plan. He gave freely of his own allowance, as did many other boys and girls. He said his father wanted to share in the gift, and probably other members of the church would like to help, too. Mike and three other children formed a committee to prepare a poster explaining the plan. They put it up in the entry of the educational building and took turns staying beside it to explain the plan to interested persons. No one was quite so thrilled as Mike when the amount given was enough for the planting of fifteen trees.

It is important to remember that Mike's father and mother had been deeply interested in the unit. They had attended the service in the temple and the sharing program at the close of the unit. The father said to Mike's teacher: "We are so glad that we took Mike to the temple. It was a wonderful experience for a family to have together. I shall never forget how stirred I was when the rabbi blessed those little five-year-olds just entering his religious school. There was a lump like an egg in my throat when he prayed, 'May you know peace in your lifetime.' With three boys of my own that has become my prayer, too."

One Sunday many weeks later, as the class was telling a new pupil about their gift of trees, Mike leaped to his feet.

"Say," he said loudly and angrily, mentioning a radio program, "they interviewed a guy who was on his way back east

28

from California. He said he meant to live in California the rest of his life, but he couldn't stand so many 'kikes.' My mother and I just hoped the M.C. would tell him off, but he never said a word. I'll bet ——— would have," and he named the well-known master of ceremonies of another radio program.

"What do you think ——— would have said?" asked the teacher, "or what would you have said if it had been your program?"

"Why," Mike stammered a minute, "I would have told him that all the people in America are Americans. No one should call names like 'kikes.'"

"But even Jewish people say that some Jews are kikes," protested another boy. "What about that?"

"Yeah, I know," Mike retorted, "but some people who aren't Jews are 'kikes,' too, if you mean that they don't know how to act decent. That man was trying to make people believe that all Jewish people are like that. They aren't. You didn't go to the temple with us, or you would have seen a whole church full of nice, friendly people. My father is sure glad he went. He says he really felt like God is great and good when he was reading all those prayers from the prayer book. He still talks about how those people loved their children and were proud of them, and about the prayer the rabbi prayed when he blessed the little ones. Don't you tell me all Jews are 'kikes'!"

Although the unit on "The Homeland of Jesus" had lasted only two months, interest in it had continued as the giving for the memorial trees went on through the winter months. Children were still acquiring new ways of thinking, feeling, and responding, both to Jesus' homeland and to his people. All through this time Mike was growing. He was growing because of what happened Sunday by Sunday in his church-school experience. He was growing because his parents were growing with him, because the church in its concern for

29

Mike and his family had provided experiences which were making that home a good environment for acquiring Christian ways of thinking and feeling. He grew a little more as he took a firm stand in the presence of his classmates, one of whom did not share his convictions.

Suddenly on the radio Mike and his mother were challenged by a word which they would scarcely have heard a few months earlier. Now because of the growing which both had been doing, they took notice. They responded in a completely different way than they would have done previously. They had learned, and this experience would help them to go on learning in this area, as they were challenged again and again by prejudice, intolerance, and unchristian speech and action.

This is not a unique or an isolated experience. It *happened within the framework of teaching materials* provided by a denomination for use with its junior children. It will happen again and again in churches where teachers think of learning as growing and changing, where they think of teaching as planning and guiding the experiences through which children learn, where they study their lesson materials as plans for helping children to grow in the Christian faith.

For Further Thinking

1. From the true story of Mike and his class can you formulate a good definition of teaching? You may wish instead to make a list of the ways in which the teacher probably guided this group of boys and girls.

2. Discuss the common questions of teachers given at the beginning of this chapter in the light of these statements:

Learning is from within. "No one can learn for Johnny."

Ceaseless activity is the universal characteristic of childhood. It is the "built-in" provision for physical growth and development. It provides the experiences through which mental and social growth take place.

"We cannot educate anyone. We can only expose him to educative experiences."

3. Formulate several questions which might be asked by a person who needs help in his work with boys and girls, but who is beginning to understand how learning takes place and what teaching is.

CHAPTER THREE

Purpose Is Important

AT SOME TIME each of us has had to do something for which he could see no reason. It is a bewildering, frustrating experience, one which we seldom wish to repeat. The desire to act with a purpose is strong in all of us.

Yet in many churches teachers go about the important task of helping boys and girls to respond sincerely and wholeheartedly to the Christian faith, understanding only in the vaguest way what the end results are supposed to be. Boys and girls, with more or less docility, follow routine procedure in department or class. The Bible is read, material in study books is consulted, occasionally the class carries out some other suggestion from the teacher's text, but all too often no one knows why any of this is done. The group does not move forward with energy and enthusiasm toward the realization of goals which they have established for themselves and which are therefore important to them. The teacher does not experience the satisfaction of recognizing Christian growth in individuals or in the class. How can he unless he knows what kind of growth he is looking for?

For effective teaching it is necessary to have a sense of direction. The teacher-guide must know where he is going with his boys and girls in their Christian growing and changing. Everything he does in preparation, the way he guides discussion, and all that takes place in a session should depend upon what he hopes to accomplish. Left entirely to chance, with no known result anticipated, the mixture of stories, Scripture, conversation, and activities which make up a class session is apt to be as fruitless as would be the baking of a woman who did not know whether the result was to be cake, pie, or bread. The teacher has both general and specific goals. He plans materials and procedures which will result in specific kinds of changed thinking, feeling, and responding. These are determined by the goals for a given unit and for a session within that unit.

The Eventual Goal of Christian Education

Goals for units and for sessions must be seen in their relationship to the ultimate purpose of all the Christian guidance we give to children, both as parents and as teachers. Our eventual goal is that each child shall become an individual who increasingly understands God's purposes and plans for men, and tries to live his life in harmony with them; that when his experiences and his growing maturity have made him ready to do so, each child shall accept Jesus Christ as Lord and Master, the supreme guide for his life. He shall choose to be guided by the deeds, the teachings, and the spirit of Jesus in his understanding and worship of God, in his daily conduct, in his attitudes toward all men and his relationships with them, in his use of the resources at his command, whether these be abilities, time, money, or influence.

The Curriculum of Christian Education

Both before and after the individual has made this supremely significant choice of a direction for his life, the process of Christian education goes on. As long as we live, we are growing and changing. We are learning. Being guided by the deeds, the teachings, and the spirit of Jesus Christ is a lifetime experience. From earliest childhood to the last of our days we may have:

A growing awareness of God

A growing understanding of how God guides us and of his relationship to all the experiences of our lives, both joyful and sad

New insights into the meaning of Jesus for us as individuals

33

Keener awareness of the ways in which we need to grow more Christlike in character

Richer opportunities to participate in the life and the work of the Christian Church and greater satisfactions as we do so

A growing sense of responsibility for helping to make the spirit and influence of Jesus felt in our community, nation, and world

Ever-increasing satisfaction and help in our use of the Bible as a guide for our living

Around these goals, basically the same for all ages of Christian learners, is built the curriculum of Christian education. Each Protestant denomination has such a curriculum for its people. It might be defined as the sum total of the courses of study offered in the educational program of that church. Just as in the public school, each course is built upon the learnings of the students in the previous years of that same curriculum.

For You to Do

Study a chart picturing the curriculum or the resources for Christian teaching provided by your denomination.

Compare the ways that goals are stated for each age group. Are these basically the same, with each succeeding age level indicating some expected growth?

In the junior years what progress may boys and girls make as they study courses planned for them in the denominational curriculum?

Units Have Specific Goals and Purposes

In the years of nine, ten, and eleven growing persons are much alike in the ways that they approach learning. Because we know something about these common characteristics, we can state purposes and plan experiences in terms that will be meaningful to these children.

This is an age when boys and girls are trying to understand the world and how to live in it in terms of reality. As younger children many of them were concerned with things as they imagined, or wished, or felt them to be. Now as older boys and girls they want to know what things and people are really like. Real places, real people, real objects, real experiences, intrigue them. Their learning about religion needs to be in terms of the objective, the concrete.

As in the earlier years of childhood, we must continue to provide vivid, firsthand experiences. Little by little these help boys and girls to put meaning into the words and phrases which are symbols of our Christian faith. When such experiences are not provided, when children "learn" these terms merely from hearing them spoken and seeing them in print, they will use them with little more meaning than a parrot attaches to the words it speaks so glibly. The experience with their minister helped Donnie, his fellow juniors, and their teachers to build new meanings for the word "worship" and for the phrase "God's revelation of himself to men." Similarly through a variety of purposeful activities and experiences "Christian service" and the "Christian Church" will become richly meaningful. Eventually the words may awaken vivid pictures of Christians in all lands worshiping God in all kinds of places, of Christian persons giving help and love to all conditions of men in the name and the spirit of Jesus Christ. These words may even become a challenge and a summons to the service of our fellows, but only when experiences have helped us to find joy and satisfaction in such service.

Many boys and girls are great readers of biography. They are eager to find out about the experiences of Jesus' life. They enjoy the life story of Paul and of Old Testament persons. Because they, too, live adventurously at home, at school, on the playground, and in the world of books and radio and television, they thrill to the deeds of that host of Christians who have adventured for God in more recent times.

The eager interest of junior girls and boys in places and peoples makes this a period for rich learning in Bible lands and backgrounds. Here the junior child's intense interest in details becomes apparent. Constantly we are made aware of the logical, concrete nature of his thinking. A fifth-grade class, beginning a study of Palestine, listed these things they wanted to know:

Where it is and how it looks

What is happening there now

What has happened there

What the ways of its people are

About its towns and cities

About its religion

About its language

About its products and its markets

About its buildings, especially its churches; how they look inside

About its animals

The work of its people

The songs of its people

The outward reach of juniors is indicated by their eagerness to be in groups, to work in groups. This is a highly social age, as every parent and teacher knows. To belong to a club is almost as necessary as food, and food is an absorbing interest. These boys and girls respond well to group thinking and working, to controls established by the group. They also desire to be a part of adult life, to share in the varied experiences which make up the culture of the world and the people about them. Important at this age are the units of study which help juniors to participate in the life and the fellowship of the church. Many will be eager to enter into full relationship as members of the church. However, pastors and other leaders experienced with juniors know well that such young church members will need careful, continuous teaching. They must be helped to participate more and more fully in the church fellowship if this step is to have lasting importance for them. Juniors define objects in terms of what they do, how they work. The church will have meaning for them in similar terms.

For You to Do

Select two units in the junior course of study that you are using. Can you explain how their goals show understanding of the ways that juniors think and learn?

Activities and Materials Have a Purpose

If the purposes of units and sessions are to be realized, each piece of material, each activity, and each experience selected for a session must have a purpose recognized by the teacher as contributing to his larger goals. Other experiences which grow out of the interests or needs, the thinking and planning, of the boys and girls will also be guided with these goals in mind.

In the land and time in which Jesus lived it was unique that he should value and serve each individual—a little child, a blind beggar, a sick woman, a Samaritan, a thief upon a cross. He was seeing all persons through the eyes of God. He was placing upon all men God's valuation of them and asking them to be worthy of God's high regard. To help boys and girls grow into this kind of Christlikeness is one of our purposes. We plan for children to have experiences through which they can see this spirit in actual practice. With our juniors we visit the Goodwill Industries. We hope that the juniors will discover for themselves that here the spirit of Jesus is at work in the community today.

In advance we talk over with the superintendent of the Goodwill Industries our purposes for the visit. After we have seen the many kinds of work being done by handicapped persons, he tells us about a few of these people. Our juniors, who care so much that they look like, dress like, and act like their own "gang," are especially interested in a young woman whose face is badly disfigured. When the Goodwill Industries came to her help, she was hiding away, hating her face and wishing that she were dead. Now she is working her way out of despair as she finds that here she is useful, respected, and valued. The Goodwill is gradually finding gifts of money which will make plastic surgery possible for her.

In the next class session as our boys and girls talk over their experience, the group decides to help with this fund. When the operation is performed and the juniors receive reports of the girl's growing self-confidence, they experience satisfactions which will lead them to seek other chances to serve as Jesus served. With new understanding they read the stories of Jesus' love for the sick, the blind, and the leper.

On the other hand, it is possible for juniors to visit a Goodwill Industries as sightseers, to come away having learned only that in this place one's castoffs are reconditioned by persons too handicapped to work anywhere else.

Both groups apparently participate in the same experience, but it leads to far more growth in understanding, in Christian attitudes, and in desirable ways of responding for one group than for the other. The difference lies in our understanding of purposes for the trip. We give better guidance to the experience when we know how it may help to realize the goals of Christian education.

For You to Decide

In the session following your visit to the Goodwill Industries, which of the following songs would you use with the class? Why? Would you or would you not use both? Why?

1. "Jesus, Jesus, Jesus,—
   Sweetest name I know,
   Fills my every longing,
   Keeps me singing as I go." [1]

[1] By L .D. Bridgers. Copyright, 1938. Renewal. Broadman Press, owner. Used by permission.

38

2. "O Master of the loving heart,
The Friend of all in need,
We pray that we may be like Thee
In thought and word and deed." [2]

Another group of boys and girls is engaged in a study of the life and teachings of Jesus. The pupils are beginning to develop a connected picture of the events of his life. They are slowly growing in understanding of what his life meant to persons who knew him in Palestine. On that last journey up to Jerusalem they go with him into the town of Jericho and find Zacchaeus, the tax collector, so eager to catch a glimpse of Jesus that he climbs into a tree to see over the heads of the crowd. They experience a little of his amazement and excitement as Jesus informs Zacchaeus that he wishes to eat with him, a despised tax collector. The story pictures the wonder of a man whose whole life direction was changed by a few hours spent in the company of Jesus. Then a well-meaning teacher, but one who has not considered what may happen to juniors through the use of this story, introduces a catchy song, "which children always love," she says, about the little man Zacchaeus "up a tree."

Perhaps never again to those children will the story of Zacchaeus mean a changed life which still today exemplifies the power and wonder of Jesus' influence upon men. Rather, the silly doggerel of the song will flash into their minds at the mention of Zacchaeus, and they will picture a dwarflike figure clambering from his tree perch to entertain Jesus. Even the goals of the unit are set back as the juniors' fine discoveries about Jesus' life and influence are deflected by a ludicrous mental picture.

Knowing what our purposes are for the Christian growth of persons and then selecting and using only materials which

[2] Copyright, 1927, by Calvin W. Laufer. From *Hymns for Junior Worship.* Used by permission.

will help realize those purposes are important responsibilities of those who undertake to teach religion.

For You to Do

List the activities, procedures, and materials used in your last session with juniors. Tell the purpose for each one, in terms of helping juniors discover what, feel how, and respond in what ways.

Pupils Must Share Purposes

Boys and girls do their best learning when they want to learn and when the reasons for doing so are important to them. All of us know that our teaching is ineffective when children do not share our conviction that a certain kind of learning is necessary or worth while. Yet how rapidly they acquire pleasing table manners, over which we have struggled for years, once their social development and group experiences make good manners seem important and desirable.

In just the same way their Christian growing will depend largely upon whether or not they feel that experiences in which they participate are interesting and worth while. It is important to choose experiences for which boys and girls are ready because of their natural interests and their level of maturity. It is also important to plan ways of stimulating keen interest and genuine enthusiasm.

A public-school teacher knew that her sixth grade could grow in language arts through the planning and printing of their own newspaper. However, she had noted that when classes did it because the teacher said they should, it was done with deadly dullness. If the experience was to be productive of good learning, the boys and girls would need to feel that it was their own undertaking, from the first idea to the final evaluation.

Quietly she "set the stage" by posting samples of newspapers, by adding to the reading table stories and informational books about newspaper life, by putting up a few pictures that might stimulate questions. Then she waited, alert, for the boys and girls to react to the "props." Soon a new boy brought the paper printed in his former school. It was passed around and added to the bulletin board. The teacher encouraged discussion of its good points and asked what other features might have added still more to its interest.

This was a class enthusiastic about art. Something in the discussion led the teacher to rescue from the wastebasket several of the bathing-beauty sketches drawn endlessly by girls. These "artists" might do a style column for a newspaper, she commented. The class newspaper came into being at that moment. Soon her desk was swamped with style sketches, and with cartoons and comic strips drawn by boys. The necessary next step was organizing a staff to handle these and other contributions. Within a few days every member of the class had volunteered for some responsibility. The activity was wholeheartedly accepted and became an excellent learning experience for this sixth grade.

The teacher and the class shared a common goal—to develop a good class newspaper, one which represented their best work and of which they could be proud. The teacher, however, saw the relationship of the activity to the broad goals of education. This determined many of the ways in which she guided the experience.

Among her goals were these: to help the class have a good group experience of working together; to help certain pupils make contributions which would earn the respect of the others and so lead to these children being more warmly accepted by the class; to help the pupils appreciate the responsibility of newspapers for reporting events accurately and fairly; to stimulate some individuals to more intelligent interest and use of arithmetic processes through problems of newspaper finances and circulation; and to help all grow in written expression.

Boys and girls who visit the Goodwill Industries can find out how this agency is serving handicapped persons in the community. As their interest and sympathies are awakened, they will acquire other purposes and undertake activities which become Christian ways of responding to human need. The teacher will guide discussion, plan worship, and choose material to help the group feel that every person is of value, worthy of our compassion and our help; have a growing understanding that such help is one way to follow Jesus; and find joy and satisfaction in giving such help.

The boys and girls who listed what they wanted to know set up their own purposes for a study of Palestine. The teacher would guide their search for information and lead them to make use of it in ways which might help them to think of Palestine as a real place where the Bible came to life; read certain of the Psalms with new understanding and appreciation; find significance in some Old Testament ways of worshiping God which are still followed by Jewish neighbors.

In one unit centering about Old Testament characters, the activities suggested were drawing, painting, or dramatizing events; writing or telling stories. To do these things, the boys and girls would need to acquire knowledge about these persons and decide what was significant in their lives. Therefore the activities would be valuable ways of learning. After the story of Abraham, the teacher called attention to James 2:23. Here, thousands of years after he lived it was recorded that Abraham was honored by being called the "friend of God." She asked how we honor people today and wrote on the blackboard the suggestions of the class:

By giving them good names (Father of His Country)

By naming places for them

By writing books about them

By making plays about them

By gifts made in their honor

This led the class to find out why other Old Testament characters deserved to be honored and to choose a way to honor each one. Through her guidance of their study and work the teacher tried to help the juniors discover how early

Hebrew leaders grew in their understanding of God and their faith in him as they met everyday experiences; appreciate the courage and pioneering spirit of these leaders; and begin to feel that they might grow as leaders by trying to meet the experiences of every day with faith in God and love for others.

For You to Think About

Could you help the teacher of juniors who said, "I don't seem to know how to get activities started in my class. The teacher's book says it would be a good plan for the juniors to make a frieze in this unit. I say to the class, 'Wouldn't you like to make a frieze?' They all say, 'No!' "

43

CHAPTER FOUR

Toward a Better Understanding of Our Teaching Materials

THIS CHAPTER IS PLANNED as a guide to the study and growing understanding of teaching materials for junior boys and girls. The statements here made may, or may not, be true of courses of study which churches sometimes substitute for those of their own denomination. If you are using courses prepared by concerns not connected with a denomination, but commercially engaged in publishing for Sunday schools and vacation schools, it will be interesting and profitable to study these by the standards which denominations set for themselves in the preparation of teaching materials.

Understanding and Accepting the Christian Faith

The gospel is the good news that God's love for men is beyond our full comprehending, that it far surpasses even the love of the best human parent for his child. The Christian faith asks us to respond to God's love first by accepting it. Then, as we let its bounty flood our lives, God's love overflows into every experience and every relationship. We become channels through which that love is made known to others. Through us it influences and changes society.

Through Jesus' life, through his teachings, and through his ever-present Spirit we discover how we, too, may open our lives to God until little by little we find ourselves growing into this same Christlike relationship with him. The desire awakens within us to honor God by right living. We find God's love flowing out through us in good will toward others, in compassion for the suffering and needy, in the urge to give ourselves to the causes of righteousness and justice in the world. So does Jesus become our friend, our leader, our guide, and our Savior.

The curriculum of the church seeks to lead each of us, step by step, into such a relationship with Jesus, and as a result of that relationship into living ever more completely and wholeheartedly as the children of God. It must never be considered simply a "body of material" to be learned, nor a set of principles to which we give assent in words. Rather, the curriculum, solidly based upon the needs, the experiences, and the growth of persons at each age level, opens new avenues toward understanding God's love and how God's will is to be done through us. It leads us to examine more and more areas of our daily experience and of the social order in which we live so that the light of Jesus' example and teaching may shine upon them.

The courses of study for junior boys and girls help us to guide them in taking the steps for which they are now ready. These older children have a growing ability to read. They have begun to understand time and change in terms of history. They are now able to increase their knowledge and understanding of God, of Jesus, and of the Christian faith through a more connected and comprehensive use of the Bible.

At this age boys and girls eagerly accept the standards and goals of persons whom they admire. This leads us to introduce them through the curriculum to men and women of the past and present who have truly committed themselves to God. Especially do we seek to bring each one of them face to face with the Jesus of the New Testament so that they may begin to measure themselves by his example. Because they are taking increasing responsibility for their own conduct, we try to help them discover and choose to use Christlike standards.

We know their strong need for "belonging." We want them

to be important, contributing members of groups that are Christian in viewpoint and in goals. The curriculum seeks to help them sense the power and worth of Jesus' influence as their understanding of the church and their participation in its fellowship grows.

These boys and girls are reaching out with eager interest into all the world. The curriculum provides experiences through which they may feel themselves belonging to a world-wide fellowship of persons bound together by God's love, and recognize that they are brothers and sisters of mankind, for all are within the family of God. It offers opportunities for them to help make God's love known to those of every race and nationality.

Junior boys and girls actively seek information about every realm of human knowledge. This curiosity, this urge to know, opens the way for Christian education to help them consider God's plans for the world and for mankind. It challenges them to seek ways in which Christian persons may work with God in his plans.

New thoughts, ideas, and discoveries may be lifted up into Christian convictions and faith through experiences of worship. Through worship good resolves may be sparked into action. Hence the curriculum includes the study of meaningful worship materials. It helps us to guide boys and girls in experiences of group worship and to lead them into the early steps of what we hope will become a rich, continuing devotional life.

For You to Do

In your denominational curriculum for junior boys and girls, try to decide how each unit seeks to bring boys and girls face to face with the gospel, to help them grow in the Christian faith. You may match the units with the above statements about needs, interests, and abilities of juniors which are considered in the planning of curriculum for them.

Why Use the Teaching Materials of Your Denomination?

1. A denomination provides a curriculum for its people, the sum total of all the courses of study used in a church. The course of study for each age group is built upon the learning of these pupils in previous years. Hence a denominational curriculum has continuity. Progressing from department to department, boys and girls, youth, and adults will have a growing experience in Christian thinking, feeling, and living. When this growth is interrupted by the substitution of other materials, pupils may hear some few Bible stories repeated to the point of boredom, while at the same time important areas in their Christian experience are left blank. To see how inevitable and how undesirable this is, let us imagine the effects upon the curriculum of a public school if each teacher used only units he especially liked, or methods of teaching long outmoded, simply because he had been familiar with them as a child.

2. The curriculum of a denomination is based upon the best thinking of that church concerning the Bible and concerning Christian faith, message, and practice. It interprets the denominational doctrine and practice. It will not throw learners into confusion by sharply contrasting points of view, as often happens when a church selects its courses of study from a variety of sources.

3. A denomination has so deep a concern for its people and their spiritual growth that those responsible for its educational program make every effort to provide the best possible teaching materials for all age groups. Because the teaching of religion must challenge the best thinking of all learners, denominations cannot afford to plan materials which require little or no time and study on the part of teachers. Because learning to understand and to do the will of God represents man's highest goal, materials which help men move toward this goal need to be worthy of respect in content, in workman-

47

ship, in appearance. It is, therefore, unthinkable for denominations to provide teaching materials which are "easy" to the point of merely reading or telling a Bible story and asking some questions about it. Materials of this kind are cheap both in price and in appearance.

4. Denominational curriculum interprets the missionary program of that church as no other curriculum material can do. The widespread evangelistic outreach of a denomination is included only in the curriculum prepared by persons who can interpret that outreach.

For You to Do

1. Prepare an exhibit of materials provided by your denomination. Group and label these so that the teacher of one grade in a large junior department, or of one class in a group-graded or small-church situation, the person responsible for missionary education, the junior workers in vacation school, the pastor preparing for a church-membership class, and those interested in junior camping and in weekday or additional sessions with juniors will know what materials are available to them. Remember that the Bible, the picture sets, teachers' magazines, and story papers are needed by all.

2. Compare the junior story papers with the units now being used in your Sunday church school. Report on ways that the story papers lift up the purposes of Christian education which are goals of current teaching units. Demonstrate how to clip, mount, and file such resource materials as poems, hymn stories, pictures, and suggestions for class activities.

3. Prepare a "sales talk" for your denominational children's workers' magazine.

How Do Teaching Materials Take Form?

All of us may help in creating our curriculum. Editors are always interested in the reactions and point of view of local church people. The editor in chief of one denomination spoke for other great Protestant bodies when he said:

Our curriculum is not prepared by a handful of editors working alone. Parents give us counsel concerning the needs of children in the home. Preachers and local church-school workers meet with editors to set forth the needs of persons "at the grass roots." Laymen in all walks of life share their judgments with us, as well as church women, missionaries, scholars in the field of Bible and the Christian religion, officials of various church boards, and workers in the local church carrying Sunday by Sunday teaching responsibilities. All these co-workers point out the definite needs to be met as we labor together at the task of providing the literature.[1]

Through a denomination's curriculum committee the thinking of all these persons is brought together, organized, and evaluated. It may lead to discussion and rethinking of the denomination's needs in terms of its local churches, of the goals of its curriculum, of the point of view concerning learning and teaching which shall prevail in its teaching materials, of its whole task of curriculum making. Denominational curriculum committees submit recommendations for changes to the committees of the National Council of Churches which prepare the outlines for the several kinds of lesson materials, for elective courses, and for vacation-school and weekday-school texts.

Members of the National Council of Churches committees are persons who hold places of leadership within denominations. Thus outlines for lesson materials and descriptions of units to be used with children are the responsibility of your own national children's field workers and editors, and of those on the staff of the other denominations. When these have been approved, they are printed for the use and guidance of the denominations.

Outlines of lesson materials represent only one part of the work going on constantly in the committees of the National Council of Churches. Subcommittees are always

[1] C. A. Bowen, *The Church School Literature of Methodism* (pamphlet). Used by permission.

engaged in special studies of goals, of children, of anything and everything which may lead to the development of more effective teaching materials. They are constantly seeking the guidance of persons qualified in the various fields of religion, as in the area of Bible scholarship. They attempt to keep our teaching materials abreast of the growing knowledge of the nature of children, in procedures which stimulate learning, and the fresh, vital insights and points of view which make religion a living experience today.

After the outlines of the National Council committees have been approved and adaptations made by denominational curriculum committees, writers for junior units are selected from persons who are experienced teachers of this age group. Editors and qualified "readers" check the manuscript and prepare it for printing. Artists and photographers make their contribution. After many months of preparation the materials for teacher and pupil roll from the press. They are assembled, packaged, and shipped according to the orders of local churches. One day they find their way into your hands and through you into the hands of junior boys and girls. What you and they do with them determines whether the curriculum of your denomination is to be an effective tool in the guidance of growing Christian persons.

There are certain basic understandings about the lesson materials which help a teacher to use them effectively.

Teaching Materials Developed in Units

Find out for yourself what this means. If you are using closely graded courses, look through the material for one year. If yours are group-graded or cycle-graded lessons, refer to the outlines for each of the three years.

How many units are included in the work of one year? How many sessions are in each unit? The word "unit" means "one." Select a unit and discover in what ways all its sessions are "one." What ties them together? Use the following suggestions:

1. Look at the title of the unit, of each session.
2. Read the purposes of the unit, of each session.
3. Discover the kinds of activities in which pupils may engage. Do any carry over through two or more sessions?
4. Is a special kind of experience planned for this unit— an experience with the use of the Bible; of helping persons in need; of discovering and appreciating God's care?

Which definition of a unit means most to you, recalling our previous discoveries about learning and teaching? Tell why.

1. A unit is several lessons about the same subject.
2. A unit is several sessions which have the same purposes.
3. A unit is a group of carefully chosen, carefully guided experiences through which the girls and boys may grow toward realizing the purposes of the unit.

The very "oneness" of a unit makes it impossible to study or teach just "next Sunday's lesson." Lesson writers try to include within one session those experiences which they think can be developed successfully within the usual limits of a class period. Since we are always teaching boys and girls, not lessons, the use which a class makes of materials and activities may mean that some groups will move on into the experiences planned for the next session; while others will need additional time in the coming week to complete work begun today.

For this reason a teacher must take time at least to "skim" an entire unit before using the first session's plans. For suggestions about ways in which teachers may help each other by planning together, see Chapter Eight.

Some readers may be asking, "Why not use materials which consist of a different topic for each Sunday?" The job of a teacher is to help persons learn and grow. Growing, hence, learning, is a slow process. Mike and his fifth-grade class spent two months slowly, gradually moving in the same direction through experiences of study, worship, fellowship with those of another religion, sharing new learnings, and responding with gifts to a need of the Bible land. Only then did Mike find himself feeling as a Christian should always feel when encountering prejudice and ill will. This could not have happened to Mike, or to other boys and girls in his class, had they studied a "different lesson every Sunday." Thorough preparation of a unit may bring the thrilling reward of seeing a junior grow and change, and this is the goal of intelligent, consecrated Christian teachers.

Materials and Activities Chosen to Realize Worthy Goals

The lesson writer is constantly asking, "*What* story, *what* picture, *what* hymn, poem, Scripture, activity, or experience will help juniors to grow in the Christian ways of thinking, feeling, and responding which are our purposes in this unit?" Sometimes this means finding the piece of material which is exactly right. Sometimes it means creating the piece of material needed to help a junior feel those desires which lead him to act in Christian ways. Often it means hours of thought about things juniors may *do* to establish the pattern of thinking, feeling, and responding which we want for them in this unit.

Not only does the lesson writer try to find or create the materials which are exactly right for the purposes of the unit, but from wide experience in teaching juniors, he tries to put these together in such a way that the experiences of the unit will move smoothly, purposefully toward the realization of goals. If teachers will ask themselves as they study, why each piece of material has been selected and why it is used at a given point in the unit, they will teach with understanding and with steady progress toward achieving the aims of their work with junior boys and girls.

Recognizing Ways in Which Boys and Girls Grow and Learn

Many teachers are disappointed in their teaching materials because, as they prepare, they look only for what the teacher is to say, the story the teacher is to tell in the session. This, they think is the "lesson"; and for these persons there often does not seem to be enough material.

For many years it has been known that all of us learn least from what we hear, more from what we see, and most from what we do. Hence good teaching materials for junior boys and girls provide for sessions filled with activity. Throughout the hour pupils are thinking, feeling, doing. They are not sitting passive while the teacher tells. They are participating in a learning experience made up of discovering, choosing, planning, enjoying, appreciating, deciding, working, judging, evaluating, worshiping, sharing. The plans are made for the boys and girls to be constantly active under the guidance of a teacher who knows the goals toward which the group is moving and who has stimulated the group to set up goals for their own learning.

Hence the teacher who is preparing to teach a unit, then week by week one session of that unit, needs to ask first, "What are the juniors to discover in this unit or in this session? How are they to feel? What are they to do?" He is then ready to ask, "How am I to help with their discovering, feeling, doing? What story, Scripture, discussion questions, and other materials am I to use in guiding them? For what activities must I have ready plans and supplies? What large, important experiences must I be prepared to plan with them?"

He understands that the "lesson" is everything which happens in the session, every experience, every activity, every piece of material, yes, even every factor in the physical surroundings and every attitude of teacher or group which causes a boy or girl to change.

Teaching Materials Are Graded

Many criticisms of graded materials come from teachers and parents who do not understand what is implied in the term "graded." These adults usually have strong feelings about certain pieces of learning, usually Bible learning, which they believe should be taught in the very earliest years of childhood. It is as though teaching the Ten Commandments to a four-year-old will serve him as a "charm" or magic safeguard against temptations. Teachers of juniors are sometimes troubled to discover that at nine or ten boys and girls cannot repeat the Beatitudes, the Ten Commandments in order, the books of the Bible, or possibly Psalms 23. Because children do not come home each Sunday recounting a Bible story which parents recognize from their own experience with the Bible—frequently limited—they fear that their boys and girls are missing out on Bible stories entirely.

To these honestly troubled parents and teachers we need to say, "All of this will come in good time. None of these teachings which are valuable are omitted in graded teaching materials. Rather, each is given a truly *important* place when the experiences of boys and girls make them ready to understand, appreciate, and put to use these truths of the ages; when these materials are the *best* ones for accomplishing our goals in the Christian growing of our children."

To show that this is true, all adults of the church, but especially parents and teachers, need to see the over-all picture of graded teaching materials. In this way they can discover just where the pieces of Bible material they think essential are used. Most denominations provide charts which make this possible. Parents will be able to understand that, while a kindergarten child can learn to repeat Psalms 23, it will be far more meaningful to him when as a junior he is studying the ways of life in Bible lands. He will be ready

54

then to discover how the faithful care of a shepherd for his sheep spoke to one poet of God's care. In the later years of childhood, as they study the experiences of the early Hebrews, boys and girls may find the Ten Commandments speaking sharply, clearly. With their rapidly expanding world, with their growing independence, Sabbath observance, profane speech, theft, covetousness, and even adultery are realities in the experience of many, as they are not in the limited experience of younger children. Yet familiarity without meaning has dulled the message of the Commandments for many an older child who now needs to learn and use them.

No teacher needs to feel that during his year or two with a group of juniors he must teach everything about religion. Already other teachers have brought these children a distance along the path of Christian thinking, feeling, and living. He is to guide them as juniors a bit farther. The graded lessons which he uses are reliable guides as to how far and through what experiences he may guide them best.

For You to Do

Make a list of ten Bible passages or stories which adults think all children should know. Find out where in the experience of boys and girls these are used in the teaching materials of your denomination. Can you explain why each comes at a given grade level? Do you agree or disagree with its use there?

CHAPTER FIVE

Toward a Better Understanding of Our Boys and Girls

WHAT MAKES Johnny show off all the time?"

"I don't believe that Sally learns a thing."

"All that Anne cares about is sitting next to Roberta and giggling at what the boys say."

"Gerald feels left out, but the other boys and girls seem to like him well enough."

"Why is Allen always late? Why doesn't he say a word or do a thing without prodding and urging?"

"What makes Pete tell such whoppers?"

"Why can't Mark enter into plans of the class? Why does he always prefer to be a 'committee of one'?"

"Why should Jim constantly make fun of other pupils' ideas, yet never offer one of his own?"

"Is there a reason why Margaret talks every minute?"

"Why does the class choose Bob or Mary or Sue for everything, whether or not they can do the job well?"

"Why can't this class settle down to intelligent planning?"

The "whys" and the "whats" show that teachers who ask such questions either consciously or unconsciously recognize a truth basic to our understanding of boys and girls, basic indeed to our understanding of all persons, including ourselves: "There is always a reason for everything we do, for everything we are."

If there is always a reason, our first step in solving a problem is to discover the reason, not to attack the behavior directly. It does no good to order Johnny to stop showing off or to ask Mark why in the world he cannot co-operate.

56

It harms, rather than helps, to call attention to Anne's silliness, Peggy's sullenness, or the group's lack of wisdom in choosing a popular person instead of an able one for responsibilities.

Our reason for noting and questioning the behavior in the first place determines in large part how effectively we will deal with it. Do we want to alter the behavior so that we will not be annoyed and so that we can more easily persuade the class to do the things we have decided are important? Is our concern centered in the fact that these kinds of behavior hinder the growing, the changing, the learning, both of individuals and of the group? Do we feel that the ways certain boys and girls act and react indicate immaturity with which we must be patient? Or do they indicate an unhappy, unhealthy state which we would like to help them overcome because we love them and want the best for them?

The teacher who frequently feels annoyed and frustrated may well examine his teaching procedures. He may need to discover how to stimulate the curiosity and purposing of boys and girls, how to plan with the group instead of for them. Perhaps he needs to guide them into wider experiences where there will be opportunity for pupils to choose from a variety of activities and to make contributions to the class plans in a variety of ways. Because we are all different, we like to do different things, we learn in different ways, and we feel that some kinds of learning are more valuable than others. The teacher who regularly purposes to have the whole class learn the same thing, at the same time, and in the same way, simply because he thinks they should, is likely to find his sessions with juniors strenuous and unrewarding.

Even teachers who normally follow a better kind of teaching procedure may find their boys and girls reacting in unpleasant and unpredictable ways when for one reason or another they hurry or push the group, or play the role of dictator. By the way in which we teach juniors we often bring troubles upon ourselves.

We deal more reasonably and more effectively with the behavior of boys and girls when our concern is for them, rather than for ourselves. The very word "discipline" has its origin in the Latin word meaning "pupil," or "learner." Hence the important kind of discipline is that which helps individual boys and girls, and the group as a whole, to learn more richly, more deeply, and with greater satisfaction to themselves.

Two kinds of study will aid us in helping our children to learn and to grow into happy, useful Christian persons— the study of individual boys and girls, and the study of their behavior in groups. For the teacher who discovers how such study can increase his effectiveness and his satisfaction in his work, there will always be new books and new magazine articles to read, new points of view in the field of child study to find out about. Best of all, there will be new children to know and new groups which challenge him to find skillful and helpful ways of guiding them.

For You to Do

Write some "whys" or "whats" about the behavior of juniors whom you know. After each question leave space to write possible reasons for this behavior as you discover them in the reading of this book or in the leadership course you are taking. Note possible ways to help these juniors, or the group, change to ways of behaving which will contribute more to their learning.

Why Are All Boys and Girls Different?

The inborn characteristics of each child are the product of one combination of parent cells out of the countless combinations which might have been possible. Since birth each of these children has had a multitude of varied experiences. Because he is himself, and only himself, he has responded to these experiences differently from anyone else, even from

58

the brothers and sisters who have shared in some of them. This in itself is enough to make him an individual.

However, the ways in which each child is different from any other are not constant, to be known and understood once and for all. From week to week the child changes. The things which have happened to him this week, or even this morning before he came to our class may make him more or less ready to learn. The differences important to us as teachers are those which either help or hinder his purposeful activity in the group.

Differences That Are Important to Our Teaching

Once we are convinced that a child learns best through his own purposeful activity, we know that our job is to help each one participate as fully as possible in learning experiences which he finds important. We can accomplish this only as we recognize individual differences and make provision for them in our planning. We can accomplish it only as we find ways to know and understand each boy and girl.

It does not greatly matter that Ben's eyes are blue instead of brown, but it does matter that Ben is a nervous lad for whom a lengthy period of sitting or of trying to concentrate on quiet study is sheer torture. We will think about Ben as we plan our unit and its sessions. We will remember that when the group studies, Ben does better when we are near enough to direct and guide his attention more than is necessary for other boys and girls. We will remember that he needs experiences with concrete objects, things he can touch, materials he can manipulate. When they study "The Homeland of Jesus," Ben and other juniors may wish to create dioramas, showing the shepherd life of early Palestine and the agricultural life of its later years. Ben will learn as he consults pictures and simple Bible dictionaries, so that he can create such scenes accurately from clay and wood, stones and real grain, clothespins and cloth.

It may not be especially important that Frank is a bit taller than other ten-year-olds, but it is important that he reads on a ninth-grade level. For Frank we will have ready a Bible encyclopedia, a good concordance, storybooks for junior-high-school boys and girls, so that he can go about his learning in ways that are stimulating and satisfying to him. Johnny's reading ability lies at the other extreme, on a third-grade level. This is important to his learning experience in our group. For him we will provide many pictures, objects to handle, and very simple storybook and picture-book material related to the unit.

When George frequently comes dragging into class after the session is half over, we will remember that all is not well in his home. This is a difference important to learning. We will not add further to the child's troubles by a sharp reprimand, but will welcome him warmly, so that he may feel loved and needed here. We will not scold or urge him to work on the Sunday when the boys and girls are anxious to finish their frieze of missionaries, and George puts down his crayon, shakes his head, and says miserably, "I just can't work on it today. I don't feel like it." We allow him to sit and watch his committee until finally he relaxes in the atmosphere of good fellowship and takes up his crayon for a few minutes before the session closes. After the others have gone, George feels free to talk a bit about his trouble. We are glad for a chance to remind him that as long as there have been people and families, some have had troubles like those of his home; but when there seemed nothing anyone could do, many have found help in remembering that God always knows, always cares, and is ready to help when people will let him.

There are sensitive children who cannot learn when sharp words linger in their minds. One day Betsy dropped her bracelet. The teacher, hearing the jangle in the midst of other confusion, asked sharply, "Who did that?" Betsy raised a timid hand, and the teacher said unreasonably,

"Betsy! I didn't expect that sort of thing from you!" Jane would have been resentful, but she would have disposed of the incident with a shrug. Betsy's eyes were pools of misery throughout the morning.

When Mary or David offer to give other juniors their parts in a play, the teacher who knows individual differences may not be especially happy at this seeming display of generosity. This teacher knows that Mary and David, so often unsure of their ability to do well, at first did want very much to be in this play. They need a chance to succeed, not to withdraw. Had it been Ross and Esther who offered their parts, it might have represented growth in their concern for other members of the class. The teacher would have been glad for them.

We will never, of course, expect all the juniors to reach the same levels of religious insight and understanding. Some from their past experiences with religion in church and home will be more able to see and to put together what they are learning now with what they have experienced in the past to make new relationships, new learnings. Knowing how limited Joe has been in a home almost completely uninterested in religion, we will be thrilled with the wonder in his eyes and voice as he says, "Just think! Some men live seventy-five or eighty years and never do anything that people remember. But Jesus only taught and preached about three years, and here we are reading about him almost two thousand years later."

How a boy or girl feels about himself in relation to the group is another kind of difference important to his learning experience.

For the first two sessions of a laboratory class George sat impassive, his arms folded across his chest, his eyes cast down. He did nothing, said nothing, and paid little attention to other boys and girls. When the class worked, he moved about aimlessly. The juniors were engaged in a unit planned

61

to help them have a growing knowledge of God through discoveries of his love and goodness in the world about them. When committees were formed to make investigations outdoors, George declined to join any of them. He went out to sit silent and alone on the church steps. The teacher joined him, but her efforts at conversation met with little response. The boy's thoughts seemed to be far away—a daydreamer, the teacher guessed.

Three committees grew out of the study, each to report on how men have worked with God to make homes, or to provide food, or to furnish transportation for mankind. Again George did not wish to participate, but a friendly boy in the second committee urged him to join this group. The members, all but George, decided that each would tell how one kind of food is the result of men working with God.

"You could tell about cheese," friendly Art suggested.

"I can't give no report," said George. "I'm dumb."

"Who says so?" asked Art.

"Everybody says so," George replied. "And I'm a mean kid, too. Everybody says so."

The teacher sat down with George, suggesting that others on the committee begin work on their reports. George seemed ready to talk a little. He assured her that he could not give a report, but something about his insistence made her feel that he would like to try. She brought simple picture books on food and homes and transportation. His reading was halting, his grammar very poor, and it seemed impossible for him to organize or even to recall information to which the teacher called his attention.

While transportation interested him more, George kept coming back to Art's suggestion that he report on how men had worked with God to make cheese. It was evident that he would like to find favor with this boy and with the committee.

The teacher helped him to think through three simple sentences about the grass and water needed by cows to produce milk, about the care that men give to their herds and their pastures, and about the knowledge and skill necessary for the scientific manufacture of cheese. The processes of cheese making, however, were clearly beyond George's understanding unless he could have visited a cheese factory and seen the operation for himself.

That afternoon the teacher saw him on the beach alone, silent. She joined him as he was putting on his shoes. They talked about the lake and the boats. Not a word was said about cheese. The next morning George was the first child to arrive. He was filled with anxiety.

"I can remember those two things about grass and cows," he said, "but I just can't get that about men making cheese."

"You do want to give the report?" asked the teacher.

"Art said I should," he answered simply; and the teacher saw how much Art's friendship and approval meant to him.

Alone with Art, she said, "George wants to give that report about cheese, but he just can't remember what to say. How can we help him? Could your committee help him?"

"Sure," said Art. "We'll tell him what to say. He can write it down and read it. We'll all help him."

When it was time for reports, George was the first to volunteer. He was eager to get his part done. Flanked by two committee members who held pictures illustrating his report on cheese, George read haltingly four simple sentences.

Because his committee listened courteously, the other boys and girls did, too. The teacher thanked him simply, just as she would have thanked any other child; and George went back to his seat with evident relief, wearing the first smile anyone had seen.

From that moment he "came alive" in the group. Now he felt that it was possible for him to learn, to do what the others did. When they read in unison, George tried to join in. He participated in a choral reading from Psalms. He brought in two contributions for the exhibit prepared by

63

his committee. Sometimes he sang with the group. He joined Art and other boys at the lake and had fun, for he was a good swimmer. He ceased to be a solitary child.

In the laboratory class he was no longer silent and unobtrusive. Indeed, his behavior was sometimes disturbing. However, the teacher and those who were helping and observing rejoiced that his acceptance in the group had made it possible for George to start learning and growing. He could begin to believe in the love of God, for he had found a measure of love and welcome in this small group studying about God's goodness and finding ways to express their gratitude for it.

Knowing Our Juniors as Individuals

A beginning step is a conscious effort to learn the juniors' names and thereafter to call them by name. Someone has said that to influence any person for good, we must be able to speak his name.

A second step is to make ourselves available to children. In the twenty minutes before or after a class session we discover what juniors are thinking about, what they are interested in doing. As they become sure of our warm interest and understanding, they bring many things to show us, many plans and ideas which may never materialize, but which are exciting to think about and talk about. The teacher who wants to know boys and girls will not merely "listen." He will respond to their interests, asking intelligent questions, sharing similar experiences of his own.

Within class sessions we will be alert to incidents and remarks which may help us understand why boys and girls are the kinds of persons they are, for we know that *there are always reasons for what each one is and does*. In our teaching we encourage individuals to express their ideas, their preferences, and their wishes. We pay close attention as the group plans activities, knowing that by their choices they will be telling us the ways in which they like to learn. As the

64

boys and girls work, we will be interested in what each one is doing. Through questions and comments we may help individuals to keep their goals always before them and to consider their own work in relation to the plans and purposes of the class.

We will be interested in juniors' conversations with one another. We will observe them wherever we see boys and girls, welcoming chance contacts on the bus, at the library, in the store. Occasionally we will plan with them the kinds of parties juniors consider fun—a potluck supper after a late afternoon of carol singing, a roller-skating party, a hike or picnic—not forgetting that whenever juniors are together to work or to play, they will be learning and growing from the Christian fellowship which a leader helps to guide.

Knowing their families and homes helps us to understand why our boys and girls are as they are. Jerry, his teacher discovered, was the only son and grandson, the only male cousin. A visit in his home disclosed that a grandmother and an aunt lived with the family. With fond complacency all the adults permitted him to monopolize the conversation and interrupt at any time. Now the teacher began to understand why he interrupted other children in class discussions, why he seemed impelled to be always in the limelight. She ceased to think of him as a rude and annoying boy and saw him as a child with a problem, which might be gradually worked out in the class since all were friendly persons. To like Jerry she needed to know much more about him. As she cultivated his friendship, she was delighted with his keen mind, with the freshness of his viewpoint about people and situations. She admired his skill in sports and his tenderness toward animals. Little by little she discovered special contributions he could make to class plans and so win recognition from the group in constructive ways.

Mickey, too, talks and talks. So does Margaret, but we know that this is a highly sociable age. We know that these boys and girls are all growing in ability to express themselves and that they take great pleasure in doing it. We observe how games often turn into talkfests, with people arguing loudly. There is little waiting a turn, little patient courtesy. We remember that this is an age when self-control, although it is growing, is still imperfect. When talking seems to hinder the progress of class thinking and planning, we encourage the boys and girls to consider this problem. The solutions they offer are likely to be very good ones and very specific, for juniors do not think in generalities:

Listen, so you won't repeat what someone else said.

Don't keep saying the same thing over, just because you think it is a good idea.

Take turns.

If you have said a lot, let someone talk who hasn't said anything yet.

Tell your idea to the class, not to your neighbor.

Stick to the subject.

The teacher recognizes honest efforts to abide by the rules and encourages the boys and girls to do so. He is good-humored and patient. That helps the members of the class to be good-humored and patient, too. And so together they create a relaxed atmosphere of friendliness and approval in which even the sensitive and nervous ones can learn and grow.

Knowing About the Group

Some classes are steady and hard-working, with well-defined goals. They enjoy the opportunity to help plan and direct their own learning. Others, like individual juniors, are less mature and need a different kind of guidance. Here, again, there are always reasons. The reasons, if we can discover them, indicate ways to guide that will be most helpful in the Christian growing of the group.

Some classes have had little experience with solving their own problems and setting up their own goals for learning.

They need a gradual introduction to independence, with larger and larger opportunities for choices and for self-direction, as they show themselves ready. We would not expect this kind of group to decide upon the making of a movie with pictures and script as the most interesting way to learn about the life of Jesus. They probably could not carry such a prolonged activity through to a satisfying conclusion, even if the idea appealed to them. Instead we might challenge the group imagination with vividly told incidents from the life of Jesus, then most informally "pretend" that we are the people of that land and day. How would we feel about Jesus? Has he done something special to help each of us? What would we say about him? How would we tell our families and friends about the things we had heard Jesus say or had seen him do? Through the use of "imaginative play" we would guide this less mature group to think purposefully, to give their full attention to a problem. We would use the Bible, pictures, and interesting, well-illustrated books on Bible background to help the juniors make their imagining more real, more true to the facts and the times. We might help them to choose a few incidents which in their opinion give the best picture of Jesus, and work on these until they can share them as simple dramatizations with another group. A hymn, a poem, a choral reading, of the teaching found in Matthew 5:43-48 would round out the dramatizations. Through such group activities these boys and girls would grow in ability to set up purposes and work together toward their realization.

A key to understanding our class of juniors may be the discovery that they are following a certain kind of leader or that the group has certain standards which determine whether a boy or girl shall be accepted. In one group the person admired and followed was a boy who openly flouted adult guidance at home, at school, and at church. Needless to say, it was a group difficult to guide until the teacher began to win his friendship and to help all the juniors to recognize and value some other kinds of leadership. No teacher can depose one boy or girl leader and set up another in his place. Instead he must help each member of the group to contribute his best to class experiences, and then help the members of the group learn to appreciate one another's strong points.

Each group has a social pattern made up of what are sometimes simple and sometimes intricate relationships among the members. Knowing the pattern helps us to understand and guide the boys and girls. Who are the members of the small groups within the larger one? Which children always sit together and visit together? Who are the most sought-after persons? Who are the left-out ones? Who are favorite working companions? Who are never chosen or are a last choice? By what standards are boys and girls awarded popularity in the group? Are these worthy standards? Does the group need to find some others that are intelligent, more just, more Christian? How can the left-out members of the group be helped to find approval from others? How may some of the well-accepted ones be guided to understand the problems, needs, and desires of those who are not accepted, and to help them into more satisfying relationships within the group?

All efforts of the teacher to understand and guide both individuals and groups have strong roots in the teachings and practice of Jesus. When the rich young ruler sought him out, eager to claim eternal life but not knowing how to find it, Jesus looked into the goals uppermost in the young man's experience and pointed out the way. For all the lowly, common folk of Palestine whose practice of religion could not meet the standards set up by the scribes and the Pharisees, Jesus gave another set of standards for "belonging" in the kingdom of God—the Beatitudes.

When we help boys and girls to establish within their own group a warm fellowship where every member is liked for himself and appreciated for what he contributes to the class experience, our teaching is following that of Jesus. We are developing the "good climate" in which each child, and the whole group, can grow toward the goals of Christian education. In such a climate the curriculum comes to life in the experience of the learners.

CHAPTER SIX

When We Plan a Unit

A UNIT OF YOUR teaching materials represents one small area in the great field of religious knowledge. It is an area in which you as the teacher hope to become competent to guide the thinking, the developing attitudes, and the Christian responses of junior boys and girls. It is an area in which you may learn and grow in Christian understandings and attitudes right along with your pupils. The only good way to begin preparation for a unit is to read the entire unit thoughtfully and inquiringly. Some teachers like to read all that is in the pupil's book first. Others prefer to read first the introduction to the unit in the teacher's book or "helps." Here they discover the purposes of the unit, the ways in which juniors may change and grow during its sessions, and what they will be finding out and doing as they learn. After the introduction many teachers read the pupil's book or quarterly, then session by session the plans in the teacher's material. In courses where the pupil's material is separated into "lessons," it is interesting to read one lesson from the pupil's quarterly, then the teaching plans for that session, and so on through the unit.

Since preparing to teach is an experience of study, put your own study habits to work at the job. Your first purpose in reading the whole unit is to get interested in it, so that you will wish to share it, to feel that it is worth spending time with, important to the growing Christian experience of boys and girls in your group. As you read underline or make notes of discoveries which seem important and interesting.

Give special attention to the Bible material, some of which will be "key learning" in this unit; for the Bible is our major textbook in practically all units of the curriculum. Find and read the references, then read the background material which will help you to understand the references and make them meaningful to boys and girls. This background material represents hours of study on the part of lesson writers. It brings to you the best thinking of scholars in the field of the Bible and of Christian knowledge and experience. It helps you to grow as an adult, even as you prepare to guide children.

A Study Suggestion

The paragraphs below under "Principles to Follow in Planning a Unit" are numbered. The next section, "From a Teacher's Notebook," tells how one teacher used these principles in preparing to teach a unit. Here, too, the paragraphs are numbered to show how each principle guided a particular part of this teacher's planning.

Principles in Planning a Unit

1. Begin your preparation by asking not what "you are going to present," or "put across," but what it is that you and the juniors will find out together. This you may discover by skimming the entire unit, both pupils' and teacher's material. If you still feel unenthusiastic about the subject and about trying to teach it, read one of the books listed under "Resource Materials for the Teacher." It may open up the subject for you and make these weeks of teaching a thrilling experience for you as well as the juniors.

2. Think about the unit in the light of your pupils' past learning experiences in church and at home. Which of these can they put together with experiences of this unit to make new learnings, deeper insights, keener appreciations? What special needs of your boys and girls can this unit help meet? What skills have they which can be utilized in this unit with value and with satisfaction?

3. When you have read the whole unit, and thought about

71

your pupils' experiences, needs, and skills in relation to it, try to state in your own words the purposes of your work for the coming weeks. Remember that there are always three kinds of goals—to help juniors discover certain facts, to help them feel in certain ways, and to help them respond in desirable ways because of what they have discovered and the ways they feel.

4. Thinking of what you hope to accomplish, review in your mind the different kinds of teaching materials used in the unit. Do certain ones seem to be "key materials," to have in a special way the "idea" of the unit, as you have discovered it? Perhaps this "key material" is a Bible passage, or one certain hymn, or a group of stories or pictures used in a particular way for a particular purpose. Jot these down for special study on your part. Plan to use them not only for study in the class, but for worship when they have become familiar and meaningful to the boys and girls. In a small church or in a junior department your juniors may share these materials with other classes during the period when all join in worship.

5. Now try to decide what special ways of learning will be most useful in this unit. Perhaps directed study of the Bible will be one of the very important teaching methods used in the coming weeks. You will want to think of ways to make the juniors eager to study these passages; of ways to make this part of each session move smoothly and quickly; of interesting interpretations which will help the boys and girls to understand and enjoy the Bible material.

Opportunities for worship must always be included in planning. Worship can lift learning to the high plane of spiritual experience and deepen, strengthen, and enrich it.

Plans in the teacher's manual will probably suggest that helping the boys and girls to do one particular thing is extremely valuable *for the purposes of this unit*. Perhaps they are to make a visit to the synagogue, or bring an offering for work among migrants, or plan a gift of books which will help primary children to understand how people lived in Bible days. There will usually be some one large activity or experience like this in which the whole class will share. To make it meaningful requires careful thought and planning. You must contact the rabbi well in advance of your trip to the synagogue, write for materials about work among migrants, or find out what books on Bible background are recommended for primary children. True, the juniors themselves must make as many of these plans and preparations as possible; but the teacher must be ready to help them to plan successfully.

6. Along with this large and important "thing to do" will be other activities for individuals, interest groups, and committees. Because boys and girls are all different, because they have different interests and different skills, each will do his own best learning in his own way. Juniors learn in the many active ways listed on pages 130 to 132. Some of these will be the best ways of learning for the unit you are planning.

If you do not have a helping teacher, you may need to enlist a mother, a father, a schoolteacher, a young employed person, to work with one group on a certain kind of activity while you give guidance to another. It will be necessary to meet with this person, to acquaint him in a general way with the unit, to suggest sections which he needs to read, and to provide him with materials which will help him to do good work and have a satisfying experience with the juniors.

7. The first session of a unit confronts us with what is probably the most difficult of our teaching tasks—to help boys and girls who have no idea about what they want to learn in this area of religion to find some definite purposes which are important to them. These will give momentum to their study for the next few weeks. To some degree we keep on doing this throughout the unit, with boys and girls who have been absent, with new pupils, with those who easily lose sight of their goals, with the whole group when in-

terest lags or when the interval between sessions makes new motivation necessary.

As teachers we must remember that all boys and girls want to learn. They are made that way. Discovering how to channel their interest toward desired Christian ends is a teaching skill which comes through experimentation, through trial and error, through experience. Suggestions in our lesson materials can help us to get started on this highly creative, highly satisfying part of teaching.

At this point in the preparation of a unit you will give careful study to all suggestions for helping the juniors to become interested in the unit and in each session's discoveries. What materials in your room need to be put away so that interest will not be scattered, but will be channeled toward this unit? What materials are to be displayed, and how are they to be used to arouse curiosity, questions, and discussion? Is the room to be arranged for directed study; for conversation, with a blackboard ready to record important ideas; for individual investigation? How will the teacher proceed so that children will begin to wonder, to guess, to ask, to seek information, to think, to worship? How can anticipation be built up for what is to be found out or done in the coming session?

The purpose of this first session is always to create a desire to begin learning in this area of religion, to give the boys and girls an exciting taste of what lies ahead in the unit. At the very beginning they must experience the satisfaction of discovering something new which, put together with their past knowledge and experiences, makes for new and different understandings and relationships in their Christian experience. What happens in the first session must be interesting enough to bring the juniors back for the next session.

8. Plan to make creative use of your materials. A creative cook probably uses the same ingredients as other cooks, with a dash of something that is peculiarly his own idea or a

74

special way of putting the ingredients together so that the result is recognized as superior. So as you give close attention to the Bible passages, the suggested conversation, the story to tell, and the other activities in which the class will engage, you will be thinking about that additional something from your own experience and about exactly how and when to use each piece of material, each kind of activity, each guiding thought, so that in combination with the thinking and doing of the boys and girls who make up the class, these may be productive of the results stated in your aims for the session.

Write down this "creative thinking" which is your way of planning for the session. At first this session plan may be quite full as you "live through in imagination" the ways in which you will guide your class of juniors. In many particulars it will be like the plan in your teacher's text, but in other ways it will be peculiarly your own.

Next review your teaching plan and make a list of everything you will need to use in the session—the Bibles, the pictures, pupils' books, pencils and paper, markers to put in the copies of the Bible, chalk, chalk board. Note everything you will need to do in order to be ready for the juniors. How will you make the room say something about the unit or the purposes of the session? How will you arrange chairs, tables, and other equipment in the light of what the group will be doing today? When will you do these things so that, as the children arrive, you will have time for fellowship?

Study the materials you will use until each has a message for you. If the group is to read in unison, you can help to make the reading meaningful and beautiful by the way you lead. Decide how you hope the juniors will feel because they have heard or read these Bible passages or a certain story. Practice the story or reading aloud until you are sure that you can help the juniors to feel that way. Be clear about the meaning of each Bible passage or hymn stanza.

75

Perhaps a song in the pupil's book will interpret the experience of persons you are studying about or will help the boys and girls to put into words what you hope they are feeling. Take time to learn the song thoroughly through the week, humming the melody, thinking the words, singing them together, until you do not need a piano. Now you have made the song a piece of teaching material, like a story, a Bible passage, or a picture.

9. Rethink your plan. How does one activity or piece of material lead into what follows? If you know, then you will have little difficulty in remembering what comes first, then next, and next. Your boys and girls will move along smoothly through the session, because there is always a purpose for what they are doing. At what points in the plan do you see possibilities for worship—after the story, when you have made plans? Will one of the Bible passages have special meaning for the class right then? What thoughts might make a meaningful prayer?

Through such preparation the teacher visualizes in advance the experience of the class session. When he begins to look forward eagerly to the class hour, he is really *ready to teach.*

From a Teacher's Notebook

(Numerals refer to paragraphs in preceding section, "Principles in Planning a Unit.")

1. I am looking forward to our new unit about how the Gospels were written. Already from reading the material in the pupil's and teacher's books, I can see that we will have a better understanding of the contents of the Gospels once we discover when, how, and why each was written. No matter how many times I teach this unit, the experience sheds new light upon the messages in Matthew, Mark, and Luke. This year I plan to read the articles about these books in our minister's volumes of *The Interpreter's Bible*—to give me fresh interest in the unit and to keep me learning.

76

2. What can I count on for this unit in the past experience of my juniors? Well, from their fourth-grade study of the Bible they will be able to locate the Gospels and to find references readily. They will know that these books tell the story of Jesus, and will be familiar with many Gospel incidents and some teachings. They will be eager to find and read the Bible stories and verses they know.

Every Christian person needs an intelligent point of view about the Bible and its writing. Our new unit will begin to meet this need for the boys and girls. The juniors will bring to the study their great interest in reality. It will thrill them to discover that the Gospels are real books, written by real people for other real people to read, in a language that they spoke every day. Surely this will deepen their sense of the "realness" of Jesus.

3. My juniors must discover that each Gospel writer told the story of Jesus in a special way and for a special purpose. For Roman Christians facing martyrdom, the Book of Mark pictures Jesus as a leader of power and courage, the true Son of God. In Matthew's Gospel new Christians, both Jews and Gentiles, saw Jesus the teacher. For a day when the new religion was looked upon with suspicion, Luke showed Jesus as the healer and helper, the friend of all. Then, too, I want my boys and girls to feel deeper appreciation and love for the Gospels because in them we can truly see Jesus. A desire to read from the Gospels and to make them available to persons who may not have copies would be one of the very best ways to respond to the learnings of this unit.

4. Yes, in the Gospels we can truly "see Jesus." That's it. A key piece of material will be the hymn "We Would See Jesus." We'll use pictures with it and connect each stanza with the Gospel which pictures Jesus in that certain way. We'll use it all through the unit, in different ways, for different purposes. And that stanza beginning "For those most precious Books of all" from the hymn "For Man's Unceasing Quest for God" will probably say just exactly

what we are thinking and feeling at many times in this unit.

In our copies of the new Revised Standard Version of the Bible we shall find proof that the stories in the pupils' books give a true picture of each author's purpose and way of telling about Jesus.

5. The boys and girls must have interesting, satisfying, firsthand experiences with the Gospels in each session of this unit so that they will desire to keep on reading them. The teacher's book tells me what passages to use, how to interpret them, and when and how to introduce them so that they will have meaning. Let's see—one experience will be to study the titles, reading "good news" instead of the word Gospel, then finding out how each book begins. As I tell about the writing of Mark, the class can read in unison these verses of encouragement for early Christians who faced martyrdom. They will study three passages in Matthew to see whether Christians still need the teachings found in this book. In Luke they will find favorite stories not told in Mark or Matthew— Jesus' boyhood visit to the Temple, his stories about the good Samaritan, the lost coin, lost sheep, and lost son.

Our experiences with the Bible will probably open the way for worship in each class session. Worship will help us to express thankfulness for the Gospels. It will deepen our appreciation of them and awaken a desire to share them with others. It can strengthen our resolves to learn from the Gospels ourselves and to make them available to others.

A gift to the American Bible Society is suggested in the teacher's manual. I must plan carefully so that the juniors will wish to respond to the learnings of the unit in this way. I have a copy of the picture-cover New Testament often given to Indian children in reservation schools. I must send for copies of the single Gospels in various languages and for the cards with a verse in Braille. I will give these to the juniors as something real and tangible to relate to the work of the Bible Society.

6. No doubt this class will decide to have a play—they usually do in this unit. Last year the play got under way too soon, I think. We used that first story about the years when the Gospel was only oral, and when it was told in the little Christian groups as different people had heard it. So that was the play. We won't begin with that story this year.

It would be fine if all the juniors wanted to give a play. However, some will probably prefer to make pictures, perhaps of the three-dimensional kind that you put in a box. Other good ideas for activities may turn up. Juniors are usually full of ideas.

And of course worship, using the Bible, choosing pictures to go with the hymn, enjoying the stories, discussing our new ideas, and organizing our discoveries to share in a closing program for parents and friends are "activities," too. Altogether they should make a fine experience for the boys and girls this month. All of them must go about their learning in active ways. I know the class so well now that I can almost guess what each one will be most interested in doing. Yet when we come to our planning session, there are sure to be some surprises in store for me because juniors are constantly changing. That's part of the fun of teaching.

I must talk with Mrs. Rilling. Her work does not leave much time for study, but I'll take our "what-to-do" and "how-to-do-it" books to her so that she can brush up on peep shows and dioramas. Mrs. Rilling is wonderful at helping children to express ideas with materials they can manipulate. I am better at words. Between us we make a good teaching team.

7. Now I must think exactly how to begin. In training classes people always ask how to get juniors interested in the lesson. Well, juniors are just bristling with interest in everything. Look at the things they collect, the different movies, radio and television programs they enjoy. What a variety of things they read—everything from "space" and "science" comics to the biography of Benjamin Franklin! Once I saw a

79

public-school sixth grade alive with excitement over their study of ancient Greece.

Well, there must be some way to direct their boundless natural curiosity toward the learnings of this unit. Getting them interested is really a problem of focusing their interest. Their curiosity, energy, and activity are good allies for us. Once we get all that vigor to work finding out the things they need to know and doing the things they need to do in order to learn, the battle is won.

Pictures are good "attention getters." In our file we have one of a man, with all his materials around him, as he is getting ready to write a Gospel. There is one of Luke questioning a person who knew Jesus, and another of Paul telling the story of Jesus to an eager group in the days before the written Gospel. We have twenty or thirty pictures from which to choose to illustrate the hymn "We Would See Jesus."

But whenever possible, I like to use some kind of objects— things the juniors can see and handle and ask questions about —to channel their curiosity. I know! The books—the Gospels themselves—all the kinds of New Testaments we have today —and those I have ordered from the Bible Society—with these we can start a "collection." That is as natural to juniors as breathing. Then, as we see how the Gospels look today, we can wonder how they looked when they were first written. We'll jump right into that material in the pupils' books about how the first Gospels looked, their language, the people who read them, the materials from which the scrolls were made. That information is at the end of the unit, but this year I will use it in the very first session to interest the boys and girls.

Probably none of their parents will know about the *Koine* Greek in which the Gospels were first written. Could that be made something important enough to share, something to help carry interest over through the week?

8. *After the First Session.* The different kinds of New Testament volumes were just as interesting as I had hoped. The collection idea caught on. Frank has a red-letter Testament

to bring and Sue a small white one which her mother carried at her wedding. When I "wondered" what the first copies of the Gospels looked like, many had ideas. I wrote them on the blackboard. The teaching picture of a man writing a Gospel did its bit—the class agreed that the first Gospels were written on scrolls. However, there was disagreement about what the scrolls were made of and about the language in which they were written. When the discussion began to get warm, I introduced the pupils' books as a way to find out which ideas were right, to get at the facts. The juniors jumped at those paragraphs. The advanced readers took their chairs off in corners and devoured the whole section. I worked with those who do not like to read silently. We read only the first three paragraphs, but we talked about the discoveries we were making. When the class brought its new knowledge to bear on our earlier "guessing," we soon had an interesting and accurate picture of what the first Gospel books looked like, were made of, their language, and their first readers.

I showed our minister's Greek New Testament. Frank wanted to hear it read. Jane and Judy wrote a note asking the minister to come and do that next Sunday.

The language—that it was everyday Greek, not classical Greek in which the Gospels were written—seemed especially interesting and important to the juniors. I linked that discovery with the Revised Standard Version of the Bible, which now makes it possible for us to read the Bible in everyday English, not the English of Shakespearean plays. We decided that the writers of the Gospels would like the new version because they wanted everyone to be able to read their stories of Jesus and to understand them.

I suggested that we find out if the story of Jesus can be understood in this present-day version. First we sang the stanza about Jesus healing from "We Would See Jesus." Then Wendy, Arthur, and I read in unison Mark 1:32-38. By their nods of satisfaction we could see that the other juniors had understood it, so we sang the stanza giving thanks for the

Gospels from "For Man's Unceasing Quest for God." I thanked God for the writers of the Gospels; for all the men who had copied them over and over, and so saved them for us; for the scholars who studied and translated in order to give us the story of Jesus in English we can all understand.

Mrs. Rilling—bless her heart!—hasn't had time to read much of the unit; but she gave us the perfect climax for the session when she said, "Well, if you boys and girls have found out as much as I have today, you have learned a lot. Most grown people don't know those things about the Gospels."

So I wondered if our fathers and mothers would not be just as interested in our discoveries as Mrs. Rilling was. Off went the juniors, most of them importantly carrying their study books so that they could read those paragraphs to their families.

Sunday evening Arthur's mother telephoned. She said Arthur was insisting that the Revised Standard Version of the Bible was a "must" for every family. She wondered whether he could actually read it if he received a copy for Christmas. I assured her that he could and suggested that the whole family enjoy together the story of Jesus as it is told in Mark.

One More Assignment

Begin to plan the next unit you will use with juniors, following the outline suggested in this chapter. Through what kinds of experiences and activities will the juniors be learning? Check the list you make for this unit against the list of possible active ways for juniors to learn on pages 130 to 132.

Skim a junior unit for missionary education, church-membership class, additional sessions, weekday sessions, camping, or vacation school. Is it possible to plan for these other experiences of juniors in the church in the same way that we plan a regular Sunday session?

CHAPTER SEVEN

Guiding the Active Ways of Learning

In this chapter read first the section "From a Teacher's Notebook." It describes activities of the juniors and their teachers in the second and third sessions of the unit planned and introduced in Chapter Six. Then study "Principles in Guiding Active Learning." Compare the numbered paragraphs in each section.

From a Teacher's Notebook

1. *After the Second Session.* Our minister was wonderful today. He read and translated for us from the first chapter of Mark. I asked him to copy Mark 1:1 on a large sheet of paper and teach us to read the Greek. The boys and girls loved that. Languages are exciting to juniors.

When he had gone away, we turned our chairs to face a group of pictures illustrating Mark 1:32-38 and above them the picture of someone writing on a scroll. Just turning their chairs rested the boys and girls. Looking attentively at the picture, I said, "I am thinking about that man who nearly two thousand years ago took his reed pen and his ink of soot and gum and wrote on the right-hand column of a new papyrus scroll, 'The beginning of the gospel of Jesus Christ.' Where did the man live? Why did he want to write a book? How did he know what to put in it? Get a Bible from the shelf, take three paper markers from the box on the table, and find these three references in Mark which I am writing on the blackboard. Then you will be ready to help me tell the story."

So I told that story just as thrillingly as I could. I had

put time and study into preparing it, reading it over and over from the pupil's book, adding some details from the articles in the *Interpreter's Bible,* actually memorizing the way to begin and end it. I told it to myself after I went to bed and sometimes when I woke in the morning. A lot depended on that story. It might prove the springboard for our planning of activities. I wanted to make those dangerous days for the Christians in Rome seem real. I hoped some juniors would identify themselves with that company and feel glad when one of their number decided to write a story of Jesus designed to give them new faith in their heroic leader and courage to face death for his sake if need be. In unison, with Mrs. Rilling leading, the boys and girls read their parts of the story which were the verses from Mark.

Everyone was so still at the close of the story that we bowed our heads and used as a prayer the stanza about the Gospels from the hymn "For Man's Unceasing Quest for God."

2. "Let's see," I said, pondering. "What do we know now about the writing of the Gospels?"

The answers showed that the juniors were thinking and learning. I wrote them on the blackboard—how the books looked, the language in which they were written, the materials used; how, where, and why scholars think Mark was written; "and how that language—*Koine*—looks and sounds," quiet Anne reminded us.

I looked at the list. "We really ought to find some interesting ways to tell what we are discovering," I said.

"Give a play," suggested Esther.

"With a big fight in it between the Christians and Nero's soldiers!" proposed Steven. Instantly half the boys were fencing with imaginary swords, and the girls were saying, "No!"

I said mildly that the play committee would have to decide about that, because fights are very hard to do in a play. People usually get too excited; then the whole thing looks silly when it is supposed to be very serious. But the play certainly ought to tell in some way about the trouble Nero was making for the Christians in Rome.

Steven looked pleased and stopped fencing.

"We could make peep shows," said Robert. I asked Mrs. Rilling to tell about another kind of "picture in the box," called a diorama. Often two or three people work together on one. I do hope Robert gets into some kind of group activity in this unit.

"We could write stories," Anne suggested shyly, "and put them in a notebook."

Some of the boys made very impolite sounds at the word "notebook." Anne flushed and said that she would help with the play. She must write her stories, too.

3. I printed the three suggestions—giving a play, making peep shows or dioramas, and writing stories—on the blackboard. Anne's name went up next to the play and the story writing. In a very short time everyone's name was beside one of the three kinds of activities. It took Kathie longer than the rest to decide, but by the time a committee for the play and one for peep shows and dioramas had been formed, Kathie had chosen the latter. She needs a good teammate, one who would not think too fast and would let Kathie do some of the planning. Mary Ann would be good. I must telephone to find out why she was absent today.

Sam has been sick. I must take a pupil's book to him. He is always so regular and such a worker that he will feel lost to come back into the middle of a unit. Why not ask him to report on ways that the American Bible Society is telling the good news of Jesus today, and how we might help? I will lend him my teacher's book. Having something important to do will make him a part of the class experience next Sunday.

4. Coming back to last Sunday, once our committees were formed, Mrs. Rilling joined the peep-show and diorama group, and I sat in with the boys and girls who want to make a play.

The story about how Mark was written had dramatic

85

appeal evidently, for that is the play committee's choice of a subject. I put an outline on the chalk board to get them started:

Our Play: What is happening?

To whom is it happening?

Who is making it happen?

Where is it happening?

When is it happening?

Lots of ideas came out. Both groups were still busy when it was time to close.

Mrs. Rilling reported that, after they had consulted "what to-do" and "how-to-do-it" books, and had discussed a variety of ways to make "pictures in a box," Robert was still planning a peep show, Billy and Tim had decided on a diorama, and Kathie rather indecisively thought she would try one if someone would help her. They had made a list of materials they would need and knew who would bring what. Mrs. Rilling will send them post-card reminders. No one was sure of a subject for his picture, although Robert was thinking of a man writing on a scroll, as in the teaching picture on the wall. Mrs. Rilling suggested that they take their study books home as usual and that they read the stories about Matthew and Luke with their families. That might help them to find some interesting and important idea to make into a diorama.

We both told Anne that we hoped she would write a story. "After the class has enjoyed it, you might mount it on construction paper and put it on the bulletin board," I suggested. "Then anyone who comes into our room could read it and learn something about the writing of the Gospels. If you should choose to tell about the writing of Matthew, you could read your story to us next Sunday instead of our hearing the one in the pupil's book."

Well, next Sunday will surely be a work session. That means some special kinds of preparation if we are all to have a good time and get well along with our activities.

5. *After the Third Session.* The room was ready for work

because I set it up on Saturday. That takes time, but it does pay off when boys and girls come in, find things ready, and go to work.

The diorama committee had two long tables at right angles. That was to encourage fellowship and interest in one another's work. Back of the piano I arranged a small table with two scrolls, a low bench, two stools, a small chestlike box. I hoped that these articles would help the play committee put themselves at once into the setting of their dramatization. The hymn "We Would See Jesus," lettered on a long sheet of white wrapping paper, I hung above a table. On the table I laid a pile of pictures which could be used to illustrate the hymn stanzas. I made a friendly corner, with study books and pictures, in which to meet the pupils who have been absent, to help them find their way into the unit. Mrs. Rilling had made a poster record of our plans. Its title was wordy, but exact: "Ways to Share With Other People What We Are Learning About the Writing of the Gospels." She left blanks for titles of stories and dioramas, for the "idea" of the play, and for the names of new committee members who might come today.

The diorama committee. Robert came early and started his peep show of paper and cardboard before the others arrived. They held a meeting and added this information to the record poster:

Robert—peep show of man writing on scroll (for Mark).

Kathie, Mary Ann, Susan, Joan—diorama of teacher instructing group of new Christians from a scroll (for Matthew).

Billy and Tim (Robert offered to help them make sheep)— diorama of Luke talking to an old shepherd at Bethlehem (for Luke).

6. *The play committee.* These juniors did some remarkable work. In trying to analyze why this was so, I believe it was because Steven completely identified himself with the early Christians of Rome. That put the other children into

the play more fully than anything else could have done. As soon as I had briefed the five who had been absent in earlier sessions—Sam had read the pupil's book and was a great help —and they had chosen activities, I pulled up a chair with the group behind the piano.

"What is happening here in Rome?" I inquired.

"Terrible things!" they told me. "Christians are being put in prison and even killed."

"Why?" I asked innocently.

"Because Nero burned Rome, and now he is blaming the Christians. Haven't you heard about that?"

"Is anyone we know in prison?" I asked.

"Peter!" they cried in a chorus.

"Listen," Steven said urgently, "you are a stranger, like in that first story in our books. We have to tell you what is happening in Rome. All the Christians are here at my house."

"Why?" asked one of the girls.

Steven pondered; then his face lit up. "We could be having a party, with real things to eat!" he exclaimed joyfully.

The rest of the committee looked steadily and hopefully at me. Somehow it didn't sound just right, their eyes said, but, oh, if it could only be that way! How juniors do love to eat!

"Well," I said slowly, "you have told me such terrible things that I don't believe I feel much like a party. I'm not even sure I could eat anything."

Steven looked sober. "I guess we wouldn't be having a party," he agreed; then his face brightened a little. "But we might be eating to keep up our strength."

I love those youngsters—so earnest, but so truly children. I'll take homemade cookies to Saturday's rehearsal, but it probably won't turn the play into a party.

"Being in Rome is dangerous!" I was frightened.

"What are we ever going to do?" anxiously queried Anne.

Their ideas about what to do were fine.

"We could run away!"

"Or hide!"

"Maybe we should stop being Christians."

"We might pretend not to be Christians, but really worship Jesus in our hearts," suggested Anne thoughtfully.

"Do those sound like good ideas?" I asked Steven.

"No, we must not do things like that," he declared. "We should be Christians even if it is dangerous, even if we *die* for it!"

There was a long pause. Uncertainty filled the air.

"You may be that brave," I finally said, "but the rest of us don't seem to be. If Peter should be put to death, that would probably take away our last bit of courage."

And that's the way it turned out. A Christian who had been watching near the prison brought us that terrible news. Everyone fled to his own home, afraid to be found in a Christian gathering. Only Steven—who by now had become the man who would write the Gospel of Mark—and the messenger remained. Steven's head was sunk on his arms. His whole attitude was one of despair.

"What are you thinking about?" I murmured from off stage. "Are you wishing that Peter were here, because he would know what to say to these frightened Christians?"

And Steven took it from there.

"Bring me a roll of fresh papyrus," he ordered the messenger. "Go to the market—"

"That would take too long," said Esther, the practical one.

"That little box," Anne pointed. "It's like the one where Luke kept his notes and little scrolls."

"From the chest," amended Steven. "My ink and reed pen can be right here. I'll write down everything Peter told us about Jesus—especially about how brave he was and how he had enemies, too. That will make them brave again."

"You could be saying out loud what you are writing," Anne suggested, "you know, the first verse of Mark, 'the beginning of the gospel of Jesus Christ.' Couldn't that be the end of the play?"

It could be, and it is.

We'll work it through again on Saturday. I had hastily jotted down on a pad most of the dialogue, chiefly because it was too good to lose. The juniors helped me get it straight, each one remembering what he had said.

This is a different kind of play than I have ever seen juniors work out, and I think it is the best kind of all. Each person created his own lines and therefore his own part. There just isn't any question about who will be who. And they know the lines because they made them up. Well, we certainly do live and learn when we live with juniors and let them be our teachers.

7. *We worshiped.* First we reported our progress and filled in the blanks on the planning chart. It made us feel good to see our work so well organized. I purposely left the work Sam had done during the session for the last report. He had chosen pictures to illustrate each stanza of the hymn "We Would See Jesus." I had suggested that he do this when he seemed to be listening in on the play from the picture table, but did not want to take part in it. It is a little hard for Sam to co-operate in something he has not thought up himself. We must look for opportunities to help him over this problem in his Christian growing.

Well, when I mentioned that Sam had selected pictures to illustrate "We Would See Jesus," it was only natural that we should all sing the stanzas as Sam showed the pictures. That led us into worship. Anne read us her story about the way that Matthew probably came to be written. I suggested that we use the Bible to find out if Matthew is still a good teaching book. We found three passages telling how to pray, how to treat enemies, and about serving the "least of these" in the name and the spirit of Jesus. We read these in unison and decided that Christians still need these lessons. So we sang our stanza of thanksgiving for the Gospels. I said "thank you" for the Gospel according to Matthew in a simply worded prayer, ending with thanksgiving for the prayer Jesus taught his disciples, in which we all joined.

8. I introduced Sam's report as a possible way for us really to show our thankfulness for the story of Jesus. Quite on his own, inspired by pictures in the pupil's book, he had made a fine poster showing some of the people to whom the Bible Society ministers. Sam is one of the juniors who occasionally does something like this at home. Of course the poster added interest to his report. He was sincere and earnest as he told about the work of the Bible Society, and of course the juniors were eager to follow his suggestion that we plan a gift.

It would be possible, Sam said, for us to provide some copies of the New Testament for Indian children in reservation schools or copies in other languages for foreign-speaking Americans, or to use our offering toward the cost of a Bible in braille for the blind. On our reading table were samples of all these, even the cards with a verse in braille. After much discussion and many questions which Sam and I answered together, the boys and girls voted to bring an offering for making the Gospels available to some blind person. From their experience in another unit the juniors decided to bring just one offering in the last session of our unit and appointed a committee to write post-card reminders.

There was a strong group feeling in everything we did today. Even Sam, who had been absent for several Sundays, finally found himself caught up in it when the others accepted his report and suggestions for sharing with genuine appreciation and enthusiasm. This was one of those wonderful, occasional days when teaching juniors seems about the most worth-while thing you do.

Principles in Guiding Active Learning

"We cannot use activities in our teaching. We do not have the space or the time." Teachers who say this understand only a part of what is meant by learning through activity.

Boys and girls are learning in active ways whenever they are reaching out for information, when they are stretching their minds to make new associations of ideas, when they are enjoying and appreciating Scripture or a picture which expresses what they are thinking and feeling. A girl's sigh of content, the long stretch of a restless boy at the close of an engrossing story, tell that they were living the story, that for them it was an active experience. Juniors who twist, squirm, poke, and talk while a teacher stumbles through the reading of a story or urges them to pay attention and think what the Bible verses mean, are saying by their behavior that this, too, is an experience—an experience in boredom.

1. Making every step of the class session an active, enjoyable experience is especially important in early sessions of a unit when boys and girls are acquiring the background they must have before undertaking so-called "creative activities." Later on in the unit the good use of materials is still important, for through them developing ideas, attitudes, and resolves are fed and nourished, and learning is deepened and strengthened.

2. When the first session has stimulated active interest in the unit, when through the good use of materials the boys and girls have a reasonable amount of background in this area of religion, the teacher may help them to set up some purposes for their learning. Often these purposes come to light as the group tries to decide what they will do with the discoveries they are making.

However, it is important to remember that this may be attempted too soon, with the result that chosen activities die quickly from lack of nourishing ideas. In the first session of the unit, for example, the only activity the class might think of would be to draw a picture, probably of a man writing on a scroll since today they have discovered that the first Gospel books were scrolls. A little later, as they find that Matthew was written to instruct new Christians, that Luke seems to have sought out people who knew Jesus, that Mark may represent much that Peter remembered of Jesus, many choices of subject matter for pictures, for dioramas, for plays, for storytelling and story writing, present themselves. Now the boys and girls must judge and compare, sort out ideas and make choices. They must search for details, verify their discoveries through Bible study. As they do all these things, they will be learning richly and deeply.

For the richest learning the boys and girls need to participate fully in every step from the first suggestions of activities and the initial planning to the final evaluation of what the group and its members have been doing. The teacher may make suggestions, too, for in a good fellowship of learners he is as much a member of the group as are the pupils. However, his suggestions—like theirs—may be accepted or rejected by the class. Always he will try to help the juniors recognize the worth of each individual and the value of each one's contribution to the planning of the group. This is not only the democratic way to guide boys and girls, but the Christian way as well.

3. Activities must provide for choice, because everyone learns best when he is working out purposes that are important to him. If a group is not too large, juniors sometimes agree on one plan, such as giving a play or a program for parents and friends. Both of these are large experiences, with opportunities for many kinds of work and activity.

Often, however, the class is not so unified in purpose. Individuals differ in interests, background, and abilities. Some lack confidence in their ability to work acceptably on a group enterprise. Others need help in finding co-operative activities satisfying. This kind of readiness cannot be forced, but the wise teacher finds ways to make what each one is doing contribute to the purpose of the group. Gradually he will guide these boys and girls into satisfying group experiences.

A helping teacher makes it possible to guide more than one kind of activity and is always a steadying influence in the group. Moreover, the experience of juniors is enriched by working and learning with more than one adult. In your church there is probably at least one person waiting to be asked, one who wants to help.

4. Once the boys and girls have decided upon activities, the teacher guides so that each child may participate fully in what he has chosen to do. The extent of a junior's learning and growing will depend upon the degree to which he feels himself a part of the experience, upon how deeply he gives to it his interest and attention, his feelings, and his energies.

By questions and comments the teacher indicates that activities the boys and girls have chosen are important and worth doing. By records on the chalk board or newsprint he helps each one to be clear about his responsibilities, and helps the group to accomplish its goals. Through leading questions and guided discussion he encourages the juniors to do efficient, purposeful thinking.

The teacher guides by introducing new materials and suggesting new points of view. He helps the juniors to obtain information they need in order to move ahead in their activity. His teaching rises to a high point of effectiveness when he helps one child, or the group, to discover from a Christian viewpoint, meanings and relationships between past experiences and what they are doing and learning now. He guides when he finds good ways to use discoveries or accomplishments of individuals or committees for the richer learning of the whole class.

The teacher gives especially good guidance whenever he stimulates juniors to work or study at home. However, boys and girls need to be sure that this at-home preparation will be put to good use in the coming session. Like adults they are busy people, but like adults they find time to do the things which seem important and worth while to them. Juniors are often eager to take assignments if this will help their own purposes or plans to move forward, or if it will prove an important, appreciated contribution to the class learning or goals. Again like adults they usually need a reminder in the form of post card or telephone call.

5. The teacher guides in a most important way, but unobtrusively, through room arrangement; the materials displayed; pictures and objects; books with markers at certain pages; the open Bible; study or work directions on the chalk board; records of class purposes and plans where they will be constant reminders; the hymn, Scripture, and poems for memorizing neatly printed on posters.

In preparing for each session, the teacher needs to rethink the purposes of the unit and how these are being realized through the purposes and activities set up by the juniors. He tries to picture how far the class may move ahead in the unit today and checks progress against the unit goals. He sees that, because certain things happened in the last session, there are natural next steps to be taken today.

As he prepares, the teacher tries to see each child in relation to the unit. What will John, Mary, and Sandra be discovering today? What will they be doing and contributing to the group experience? Are special materials needed for individual pupils if they are to keep learning and growing as Christians in the unit?

In each session interest must be reawakened, and group plans must again become uppermost in importance. It is easy and quick to say, "Class, last Sunday we decided to make dioramas. Now let's get to work!" But such a summons does not mean that the juniors will be ready to do so. It is better to say, "John, just before we went home last Sunday, you had a wonderful idea about using clay for the wall in your diorama. Do you think that would work for the house that Esther and Jean want to put in theirs? Or would a salt and flour mixture over cardboard be better?"

6. We will judge the worth of any activity not by the perfection of the finished product, but by the depth and quality of the children's experience. Has something good for his growing happened to each one who worked on the frieze

or took part in the dramatization? This is the matter of true importance. We guide an activity always with the hope that whatever we say or do, whatever help we give, may make the experience more vivid, real, and satisfying to the boys and girls. For this reason we try to help juniors plan their frieze carefully. They will be dissatisfied and unhappy about it if the result is not pleasing to the eye. We try to help them remember their lines in the play and speak them with feeling so that they will be the person they represent, thinking his thoughts, sharing his experiences. Flashes of insight, of real learning, come to boys and girls when their interest and feelings are deeply engaged by the carefully chosen, carefully guided experiences of a unit.

When the play described in "From a Teacher's Notebook" was to be given for parents and friends, Steven arrived wearing without a trace of self-consciousness a most realistic corn-silk beard. While the teacher helped him into his costume, he said wonderingly, "I'll bet the man who wrote Mark never thought we would be giving a play about him or that people would read his book two thousand years after he wrote it."

"No," the teacher agreed, "but his good news was so wonderful that people still want it and need it. That is what makes the whole Bible different and lasting."

A sixth-grade girl tried to tell in verse how she thought the people of Jesus' own day felt about him. Out of her past experiences and new learnings she wrote:

> He lived like God
> For men to see!

In occasional flashes like these we are privileged to see what is happening to boys and girls. Usually these wonderful, revealing moments come in the midst of the activity, suggesting that in doing, in creating, juniors have their finest experiences of growing and learning.

But there are values in sharing with other groups in the church school, with parents and with friends, what the boys and girls have done in a unit. The interest of others helps juniors to feel that their work has been worth while. As they try to put together materials and activities of the unit in ways that will be interesting and helpful to an audience, they may find new meanings and relationships, new insights, in the experience.

"Will our program be helpful to the parents and friends who see our plays about the lost coin, the lost sheep, and the lost son?" asked a teacher.

The juniors pondered a moment, then:

"They will know that God is loving and forgiving."

"Maybe someone will come who should ask God to forgive him for something. After he sees our play about the lost son, he might do it."

"Have we learned any hymns or Scripture which might help our program to do those two important things?" asked the teacher.

Suddenly the boys and girls realized that the hymn "There's a Wideness in God's Mercy" could help. They had studied its meaning and learned to sing it well. Now they sang it with a purpose that was important. They added a prayer written by one of the group and a choral reading of the hymn "Brother of All the World." [1] Their sharing program became a genuine experience of worship for both juniors and their guests.

In guiding activities, how much help does the teacher give to individuals or to groups? There can be no definite rule. Certainly the teacher will never take over an activity and "run" it, nor will he deal out advice in wholesale lots. Instead he is "available" when help is needed and boys and girls ask for it. Never will he take the brush or pencil from

[1] *Hymns for Junior Worship.*

a young artist's hand and add telling strokes to the child's picture, nor will he add words to a young writer's master-piece. When the junior is dissatisfied with his efforts, on an-other piece of paper the teacher may indicate what would help. It is unforgivable to destroy a child's sense of "ownness" in his work.

Yet it is not good leadership to meet requests for advice or help with constant urging to "think it through yourself." Should an adult ask what we would do or what we think, we would respond honestly and freely, but always leave wide open the right to accept or reject our counsel. Juniors respond best to the same courteous, friendly treatment we give to older people.

7. In every session it is important to help the boys and girls have a sense of achievement. We must round up the expe-rience and lead on into new avenues of discovery and plan-ning. When the class has worked on activities, groups and individuals must have a chance to show or to tell what has been done. If this is not included in their reporting, the teacher will indicate how the work contributes to the larger plans and purposes of the group.

Throughout the session as juniors and their teachers work and study and plan together, a sense of oneness should be developing. This unity makes the group ready for good wor-ship experiences, as they seldom are at the beginning of the hour. In the small class or large grade, in the one-room church or the big junior department, teachers must plan to lift each session into a high moment when juniors sense that all has been done "to the glory of God."

8. By the methods of teaching we sometimes employ, it is possible to defeat our purposes for living in Christian brother-hood. When the adult leader singles out individual children to participate because they read exceptionally well, learn the lines of a play quickly and speak them loudly, or sing beau-tifully, quite unchristian attitudes may be taking root in these juniors and in their classmates. To pass these privileges

around is not the solution, for the boys and girls will still be vying for the favor of the teacher. They will be ruled by a spirit of rivalry and competition which will inevitably destroy their Christian fellowship. In a group where the cry frequently arises, "Let me! Let me! I'll do it! I'll do it!" the teacher needs to examine his teaching procedures. Such a spirit indicates that juniors do not have opportunity to plan their own activities or to enjoy rich, rewarding experiences in their units of study.

A sense of "togetherness" comes when we work in groups and make most of our contributions as groups. Group singing, choral or unison reading, dramatizations with a part for everyone, are better methods than solo work. In these all may share, even the child who does not carry a tune and the most self-conscious, stumbling reader.

When individuals do contribute—and at some time every child should do so—this should be a sharing of their own creative work. The teacher accepts the excellent report, the well-written or well-told story, the fine poster, not with praise for the ability of the child, but with appreciation for the way it contributes to the group's purposes. Once this spirit takes hold, juniors often express sincere appreciation for one another's work. Every session with juniors should be an experience of "dwelling together in unity." When each child feels himself loved, accepted, and valued, he will be able to do his best and to be his best. He will be experiencing the spirit of Christ in the fellowship of juniors.

Another Assignment

You and another member of your leadership class may pretend to be the teacher and the helping teacher in "From a Teacher's Notebook." Plan together how to organize all the materials and work of the unit so that the sharing program will be most effective (1) in helping the juniors to find new meanings, insights, and relationships in this learning experience; and (2) in helping parents and friends to understand the purposes of the unit for the boys and girls.

At what point in the program will you use the hymn "We Would See Jesus"; why there? How will you relate it to what comes before and after it in the program? What passages from the Gospels will you include; why? To what will you relate them—to the hymn, the dioramas, the play? When will you include prayer? What kind of prayer will it be? Will the gift for the American Bible Society be a part of the program? How may the actual giving of the money be made meaningful and effective?

Include in your role playing of two teachers planning together, the ways to help the juniors participate most fully in the planning and carrying out of this program.

CHAPTER EIGHT

When Teachers Plan Together

GUIDING A GROUP of eager, growing juniors may be a rich experience in Christian knowledge and service. However, it needs to be a social experience shared not alone with boys and girls, but with other adults engaged in teaching work. To establish a vital fellowship of teachers is the greatest need in the educational program of many churches. The existence of such a fellowship will attract potential workers, while it maintains the interest, enthusiasm, and loyalty of those already engaged in the teaching task.

Persons need never be lost to this fellowship, for those who are temporarily unable to teach may still meet and help plan. They may contact parents by telephone or mail. They may serve as committee members for parent-teacher sessions. They may keep abreast of their fellow teachers through reading and study, and make special contributions to meeting programs. When circumstances again permit, many will return to active teaching relationships with new vigor and real joy. In this way the children's division may build up a backlog of persons who have served, who understand the goals and procedures of the educational program and who are concerned that it shall progress.

Where such a teaching fellowship does not exist, work with boys and girls rises and falls. Under inexperienced and fluctuating leadership, policies and procedures change constantly. All too often a church finds its educational program moving in reverse, and years may be required to bring it again to the level it had once attained.

If, then, the establishing and maintaining of a teaching

fellowship is of such great importance, how may those who work with boys and girls of junior age proceed? First, let us remind ourselves that if our pupils are to grow as Christians, their teachers must be similarly growing. All persons, regardless of age, grow best in a friendly, approving atmosphere, where they feel themselves important, contributing members of a group doing worth-while things. Successful personal relationships of superintendent with teachers, of teachers with other teachers, of teachers with their helpers, develop when all are friends trying together to determine a worth-while program for this age group.

Whose Responsibility? Why Meet?

In most churches the junior superintendent or the superintendent of the children's division will be responsible for calling the teachers together. How this is done can determine the success or failure of the venture. Many a potential teaching fellowship has died before it started because a busy, efficient leader autocratically summoned the group to a meeting. To consult all members about the best meeting time takes time and effort on the superintendent's part, but it results in better attendance and more wholehearted participation.

Some churches find a more vital fellowship existing among the workers when they come together, not always at stated intervals, but when there seems a need to meet. A teaching fellowship may hold its first meetings because teachers are concerned about plans for Thanksgiving and Christmas observances, and how boys and girls are to share in the plans of the whole church for these seasons. Later the teachers may feel a need for special help with missionary-education units and enjoy thinking about and planning for the kinds of service activities from which children will choose. A need for help with a basic concept of the Christian faith may draw the group together. Before Eastertime, for example, the minister may be invited to help teachers clarify their own thinking about the death and resurrection of Jesus. Then the group may think through the ways in which these events are to be interpreted to juniors, each bringing a contribution from his own study of the unit he will be using. The superintendent of the children's division or teachers of younger groups may bring a report of Easter as interpreted for the younger ones, so that junior teachers will know upon what concepts they are now building. Planning a summer teaching schedule or getting ready for promotion offer other practical and important reasons for coming together.

As fellowship grows and teachers find help and pleasure in their group planning, such meetings are sure to become more frequent and regular. Junior teachers of the Sunday-morning church school will wish to meet well in advance of the beginning of each new unit. Those who guide the additional sessions, vacation school, junior choir, or camping experiences will think through with all the junior workers the purposes and procedures of their sessions. Only in this way can a church develop a comprehensive, well-rounded Christian experience for its boys and girls. Where there is only one class of juniors, fellowship will need to be established and planning done with teachers of younger children.

The Role of the Junior Superintendent

The superintendent of the junior department should be considered a helping teacher, not someone who orders supplies and leads the department in an independent and unrelated period of worship. The superintendent stands ready to help with the juniors in any way. He welcomes opportunities to know boys and girls more intimately, to become more thoroughly acquainted with teaching materials through occasional chances to use them in a class group, to work with a teacher and his pupils on an activity which requires an additional helper. His first responsibility is to give guidance, help, and direction to the real work of the department. That real work is always helping boys and girls to participate in experiences through which they may grow as Christian persons.

The junior superintendent and the superintendent of the children's division have a special responsibility for recruiting new teachers. They must help the new teacher to learn his job and to find satisfaction in the teaching task as soon as possible. For the inexperienced person a gradual introduction to the work is best. First he may sit in as an observer with an experienced teacher. Sometimes this will be the superintendent himself, for his concern that a class without a teacher shall still have fine learning experiences will make him willing to assume this additional responsibility until a qualified person can take the group. Moving from observer to helper and finally into full teaching responsibility enables the new teacher to feel his way, to get acquainted with boys and girls, to see what works and what does not work, and to ask questions about the policy and procedures of the department.

Most new teachers will need help with the point of view that the juniors learn as they do, that a teacher does not "teach the lesson," then "have activity" or "handwork." Few adults have had opportunity to learn through their own discovering, feeling, and doing, either in the church school or in public school. In order to make this fundamental discovery about learning and teaching, they need to see what good things happen to a group of juniors so engaged. If new teachers are handed a book and thrust into a group of children, they will naturally begin to "teach" in the way they know—usually "telling"—and it may take years for them to find their way into a different kind of procedure. The junior superintendent or a skilled teacher can guide new workers to try the better ways suggested in their materials during their first experiences with the junior boys and girls of the church.

As the new teacher participates in the regular meetings of the department, he will discover how teachers prepare to give competent guidance to this kind of learning. He will learn to plan as he plans with the other workers. He will catch their enthusiasm for helping boys and girls to do the interesting, worth-while things through which they learn best. He may bring his questions and his problems for the consideration of more experienced teachers and in so doing will actually enrich the fellowship of the group. Warm, friendly feelings rise spontaneously as we find ourselves helping a fellow worker to be more successful. It is easier to enlist new teachers when we can honestly assure them that a group of friendly workers stands ready to help them learn to teach, to assist in every possible way.

All teachers, not only the new ones, need to meet regularly for planning sessions if they are to do effective work. The benefits of such advance planning are readily apparent. To share with other teachers our plans for a unit makes it necessary to read and prepare well in advance, something we are apt to postpone too long. Sharing plans also means that materials are ready when needed. We can plan opportunities for classes to work together or with groups outside the junior department. The developing and directing of such a planning fellowship of teachers is an essential part of the superintendent's constant goal—to help boys and girls participate in experiences through which they may grow as Christian persons.

Planning Together for New Units

The junior superintendent must take time to become increasingly familiar with all the kinds of learning experiences in which juniors should participate. He must come to know the various units of the junior curriculum. This is quite possible, since these remain constant in the closely graded courses of study, and similar units may be repeated in three-year cycles in group-graded or cycle-graded courses. A beginning superintendent may be able only to "skim" the units in one quarter's work. Even this much preparation makes it possible for him to say, as he hands a teacher all his materials well in advance of the beginning date for that unit, "This looks like a fascinating unit. I want to study it more thoroughly myself because there is so much in it for all of us to learn and think about. As you read through the first unit before our teachers' meeting, will you make a few notes to share with the rest of us? We all ought to know what purposes you have in mind for your class (or grade). Select one or two of the activities you think will lead to the best learning and be ready to describe them for us. Let us know which pieces of material seem especially important. One or two usually contain the idea of the unit and therefore are good to use repeatedly."

Advance study on the part of teachers provides the necessary substance for the planning meeting. The fact that the superintendent has taken time to become familiar with the material and that he needs two or three special kinds of information from each teacher will stimulate and encourage them to give time to preparation before the meeting. However, a patient, friendly, kindly spirit may be needed before some teachers discover for themselves how helpful it is to prepare for a whole unit and come ready to make good contributions to the department planning.

When the teachers meet, the superintendent may plunge them headlong into the work of planning for new units by asking, "What will be happening in our department during the coming month or the coming unit? What will each class of boys and girls be doing?" This puts the emphasis where it belongs—upon the active ways of learning in which the juniors will engage. It also puts the teacher where he belongs, for his job is obviously to help the boys and girls do those things through which they will learn best.

As reports are given by the teachers, the plans they propose should be recorded on a sheet of paper large enough for all to see. It might well be arranged in three columns:

What the juniors will be doing:	Discoveries, attitudes, and responses we hope will result:	Materials we think will help significantly:
Grade 4		
Grade 5		
Grade 6		

Purposes come first in our preliminary study of a unit. In this planning session they may be recalled as a check upon the activities planned for each class or grade. The fourth grade, for example, may be spending much time in examining copies of the Bible. Why? With what hoped-for results? As in the experience of Wayne, recorded in the first chapter of this book, the boys and girls might experience frustration or boredom. It all depends upon *how the teacher guides this experience.* Seeing the goals of the activities makes him aware of this in another way. Key materials might include one of the Psalms to learn as a choral reading, the story of Joseph to dramatize, the hymn "Book of Books."

Thus, as the teacher of each class or grade fills in the planning chart, all have a picture of what will be going on in the department during coming weeks. They begin to *feel themselves important, contributing members of a group doing worth-while things.*

Where group-graded or cycle-graded lessons are in use, or where one large grade meets as a department, all teachers and their pupils will be working toward the same goals. Each class, however, may learn through different kinds of study and planning, through activities which have special appeal for individual teachers or which they believe they can guide successfully. Gradually, as teachers grow skilled, they will see the need for boys and girls to choose and plan their own activities. When this is done, the usual class organization based on age or school grade may be set aside, and boys and girls may work in the committees or activity groups of their own choice. Each teacher, then, will be responsible for guiding one group by using the teaching materials in ways which will result in most fruitful learning for the juniors who are working with him.

In departments where closely graded courses are used, the planning chart will show that often all grades are working in the same general area of Christian experience, even though the courses and specific goals may differ. For example, all three grades may be studying in the area of the Bible. Grade 4 may have the unit "Learning to Use and Enjoy the Bible"; Grade 5, "The Homeland of Jesus"; and Grade 6 is intent upon "Understanding the Early Old Testament." The same is true in the area of the Church.

In the small church, with perhaps one class of kindergarten children, one of primary, and one of junior, teachers of these groups may plan in the same way, using the same kind of chart. Here, too, they will find frequently that all three groups are working in the same general area, and that there are key materials carrying like emphases which may be shared by one group with the others.

Planning Experiences of Worship

Worship will hold an important place in the listing of "what the juniors will be doing" on the planning chart. As for all other activities, there will be specific purposes for worship experiences in a unit. When they worship, what are the boys and girls to be thinking? What new ideas of God's purposes may come to them? What attitudes or feelings helpful to their Christian growth may be awakened by worship? How may worship strengthen their purposes and resolves to respond to God's will and God's way?

Worship may be conducted in a variety of ways. Just as certain kinds of activity are more effective than others for the purposes of a given unit, so will some ways of worshiping contribute more to the realization of goals in a unit than will others. Our ways of worshiping may vary from session to session and even be different for each class in any one session. The guiding principle behind all our planning will be the realization that true worship is an "experience," not a "program." We hope that each boy and girl may actually feel something happening to his understanding of God, to his desires and his resolves as a Christian person, because he has participated in this worship experience.

Through a simple prayer in the class session, thanking God for some new insight, boys and girls may have a feeling of "relatedness" to the Father. The words of a psalmist, lines from a hymn, or the climax of a well-told story may help juniors suddenly to become aware that this is what they, too, believe God to be like or that this is what God expects of them. Such awareness, such insights, such molding of purposes and desires, are the reasons for worship.

Thus as they plan, teachers may decide that informal worship within the smaller class group will be most helpful in one unit, and plan for all classes to come together only once or twice. Perhaps in the first or second session of the unit the boys and girls will wish to share with other groups their plans for the unit. Then near the end of the unit they may meet to share their discoveries and their work.

In another kind of unit the learning of new worship materials will be an important activity. The teachers may set aside time in each session for all the juniors to learn hymns, work on the choral reading of Scripture, and study pictures from sets accompanying the teaching materials or as slides projected on the screen. Always the leader will be sensitive to opportunities for lifting this time of group study into a high moment when the boys and girls may become keenly aware of God. To close a unit where such a plan has been followed, the materials which the group has studied may be brought together into a more formal time of worship.

The plans for junior worship printed in denominational teachers' magazines each month often use materials from the junior units of study and are built around themes in line with the goals of these units. Many leaders of long experience use these worship suggestions quite regularly, adapting them to plans made by their own fellowship of teachers. They recognize that the denomination provides these as a part of the carefully planned resources which together make up the denominational curriculum for juniors. To use these resources skillfully, it is necessary to study them with the basic understanding that worship is an experience, usually brief, even momentary; that the materials in a "service" build toward a moment when something vivid and real is happening to the insights, feelings, and resolves of worshipers. Trying to visualize as part of our advance planning the point at which this experience may come in a class session or in a period of group worship will make it possible for us to help it happen.

Worship experiences for the class or when all come together may take form around the "key materials" of the unit or units. Often a real moment of worship develops in fellowship and in the sharing of plans between classes. A hymn or passage of Scripture which is "key material" for one group may express what the boys and girls are feeling. Thus worship grows out of experiences the juniors are having in their units of study and at the same time contributes something more to the sum of those experiences. Never should the so-called "worship service" be a separate program planned and led independently of what is happening in class groups, for this will destroy the unity so essential to the juniors' experience in a total session.

For You to Do

1. In the section "From a Teacher's Notebook" find records of what you would consider worship experiences. How did these contribute to the insights, attitudes, and responses which were goals of that unit?

2. Study the next unit you will be using with juniors to determine what ways of worshiping may be most helpful

to the boys and girls. Note carefully all suggestions for guiding the group in worship. Begin to learn materials which will be used in worship experiences.

Helping One Another

As all teachers look with friendly, approving eyes upon one another's plans, they may help by suggesting where materials can be obtained, the best ways to stimulate interest in an activity, and good ways to use what the boys and girls make and do. Resource books may be shared, experiences with similar kinds of activities recounted, and suggestions made about parents or friends who will serve as helping teachers for a class where two or more activity groups are likely to develop.

Sometimes readjustments will be necessary so that a teacher may work out his plans. How can suitable space be provided for the dramatizing which Mrs. G. believes will be especially fruitful for the learning of Grade 5 in this unit? To make that large frieze, Grade 6 will need more working space. When all teachers help solve these and other knotty problems of one class or of the department, they will be growing in Christian fellowship, in group unity, in warm concern for all that is going on among the juniors.

As teachers learn together certain of the hymns which are key materials, or work out a choral reading of a psalm, or listen to a beautiful, vivid reading of a key story, a deepening and strengthening of interest in the new unit or units may result. Somewhere in the planning meeting, not always at the beginning, there should be moments of worship. Like boys and girls, adults "need something to worship about." Participating in informal and frequently spontaneous moments of worship in their own meetings will help teachers to become sensitive to such opportunities in their sessions with juniors.

Often a teacher needs counsel about an individual child. Alice is always "blowing off steam" and usually in ways that

111

are disturbing to the group. The problem seems different when we discover that she lives under the strictest discipline at home. An older sister reacted by never having an idea of her own, but Alice is made of different stuff. Greg is very nervous. His head twitches. He comes irregularly and cannot give attention much longer than an average kindergarten child. We begin to make special plans for Greg when someone in the teaching group tells us that he is cared for by a succession of unsatisfactory housekeepers because his mother is too ill to be in the home. Betty and Bob are rough and noisy in every word and movement. We feel differently when we learn that violent quarrels over what these children should and should not be allowed to do have finally ended in the separation of their parents.

Just as in our sessions with boys and girls, at moments like these the fellowship of teachers may feel drawn to share such anxieties for their juniors with the all-knowing, all-wise, all-loving God. They pray for guidance, for a measure of that perfect love which Jesus gave to the needy ones of another day.

The fellowship meetings of teachers should be varied in program and in purpose. As classes or grades are about to begin a study of the life of Jesus, of what it means to be a Christian person, or of ways that the church is serving in the spirit of Jesus, all teachers will have their vision enlarged and their insight deepened by an able review of such a book as Edgar Goodspeed's *A Life of Jesus*. In another meeting there may come new sympathy with and understanding of children from the pamphlet by James L. Hymes *Teacher Listen—The Children Speak*. A film may stimulate the group to evaluate their own work with juniors. Viewing the Elsie Anna Wood slides picturing the life of Jesus may result in a discussion of when, how, and why certain ones of these may be used in the various units of the junior curriculum.

Possible additions to the teaching group should be discussed in every meeting. Knowing that Mr. and Mrs. X. worked with children in their former community will provide opportunity for members of the junior teaching staff to give them a warm welcome to the church, to invite them to their fellowship meetings, and to share their enthusiasm for boys and girls and what this church is doing with them. The information that John's mother is interested in her son's experiences in the department may suggest her use as a helper, either temporary or permanent, in one of the classes. In such ways as these is the important "backlog" of persons concerned in the church's educational program built up.

For You to Do

Pretend that your leadership class is the "fellowship of workers with juniors" in one church. Hold a meeting, using suggestions from this chapter and planning together for a coming unit.

In your "meeting" work together on a choral reading from a junior unit of study.

Planning for Juniors in Larger Ways

Teachers of juniors are always eager that their pupils shall live more and more widely, more and more richly, in the fellowship of the Christian Church. Gradually as their understanding of learning, of their purposes, and so of their teaching task grows, as their skill in guiding boys and girls increases, workers with juniors should venture into activities which enable their pupils to live in ever-larger relationships with other classes and ages in the children's division, with youth and adults in the local church, with groups in the community, and so out into the world-wide fellowship of the Church. Planning such experiences will constitute the main business of some teachers' meetings.

In their study of Psalms as a hymnbook related to the hymnal of their own church, Grade 4 may purpose to do some special work with choral reading. The older juniors may join

113

this enterprise to form a large chorus for certain sections of a program which is to be shared with adult groups. Learning to chant Psalms 95, to sing hymns derived from Psalms, to interpret two or three Psalms through a beautiful and meaningful reading of them, may take much of the time allotted to fellowship and worship. It is a worthy use of such time if carefully planned by all teachers. As they "worship with the Psalms," boys and girls will be learning; and the church fellowship will be made more aware of the good things taking place in the Christian education of children. The progress of the educational program often depends upon just such awareness on the part of adults.

Venturing into Christian community living, the juniors may invite as guests children from a church which because of race, nationality, or economic status has little fellowship with other Christian churches. At Christmas time such an experience may be the juniors' way of showing active good will, of making real the angels' song of peace on earth. All classes may plan together, using some of the department fellowship and worship time. Perhaps Grade 6 will prepare an effective center for worship and develop a simple program around the theme of the angels' message. Grade 5 may make an attractive folder as a gift for each guest and put inside a mimeographed copy of the Christmas story from Luke. Grade 4 may plan and serve simple but festive refreshments. Such an occasion will help juniors to take long steps toward an understanding of Christian brotherhood.

Sharing in the world outreach of the church is important for juniors. Their teachers will see that they have firsthand contacts with missionary families and with Christians of other lands who may be in the community. By exchanging letters and pictures, by remembering these other Christian friends with prayers in class or department, by gifts of supplies, by helping boys and girls to have a vivid picture of what their money gifts will do in a mission center, we make sharing the good news of God's love a real experience to juniors.

Interest and concern for all God's people everywhere must be a continuing week-by-week experience for our boys and girls. Members of the teaching fellowship will look for opportunities to give such guidance in every unit, as well as in those which are planned specifically for missionary education. They will help juniors to make discoveries about the fellowship, work, and needs of the Church in other lands. They will help them find effective ways of sharing their discoveries with other groups and of assuming some responsibility for the missionary efforts of their church. By so doing, boys and girls will be engaging in the main business of Christians. They will be sharing the gospel with the peoples of the world and joining with them in a common allegiance to God as the Father of all. This is the best way to work for a world in which God's purposes and plans will be realized.

CHAPTER NINE

Some Problems of Organization

THOSE WHO WORK as Christian leaders with junior boys and girls are called upon to interpret to the rest of the church family the needs of this age group. They must be able to explain to committees and boards the conditions under which children do their best growing and learning in the Christian faith. While no one plan can be best for all churches, still the following guiding principles can help us determine some good ways to group and grade our boys and girls, to use our building and its equipment, and to use the time available to the church for the most effective learning:

Juniors learn best in a friendly, approving environment.

Juniors learn best in comfortable, pleasant surroundings.

Juniors learn best when they feel themselves important, contributing members of groups doing worth-while things.

Juniors learn best in an experience which is "unified," where all learnings of a session are directed toward the achieving of one set of goals.

Across the country we find nine-, ten-, and eleven-year-olds studying, working, and worshiping in the five kinds of groupings: (1) in the one class of the smallest church, where three or four juniors may be meeting with eight-year-olds and twelve-year-olds; (2) in the one or two classes of juniors in small churches; (3) in a junior department with one or more classes for each of the three grades; (4) in two-grade departments, one consisting of Grades 3 and 4, and the other of Grades 5 and 6; (5) in a one-grade plan, with a separate room and staff of teachers for each school grade.

At the present time experienced leaders of juniors generally agree that these boys and girls do their best learning under the following conditions:

When the group numbers not more than twenty-five boys and girls, with a leading teacher and a helping teacher (who may exchange responsibilities in successive units), and a secretary. One of these will serve as pianist.

When the group has a room of its own, allowing twenty to thirty square feet per pupil.

When the room is light, restful in color scheme, orderly in appearance, quiet as to floor covering, and if necessary insulated against sound from other groups.

When at each session the group spends a full hour or more in their own room, engaged in activities of study, work, worship, and fellowship planned with their own teachers.

When furniture is attractive, comfortable, sturdy, and scaled to the size of juniors, with chairs fifteen to seventeen inches high and tables ten inches higher than the chair seats.

When furnishings of the room include provision for wraps, adequate storage space for supplies; a good-sized chalkboard; mounting space for displaying pictures, other materials, and the work of the group; a piano.

When there is a table of good proportions against a screen or wall hanging to be used as a center for arrangements which may direct the group's attention to worship.

When provision is made for using projected visual aids in the room.

When the atmosphere in a session is one of natural, friendly, and informal Christian fellowship.

When there is always flexibility in room arrangement, time schedule, teaching procedure, and leadership—all of these depending upon the plans and purposes of the group for a session.

A few churches do provide most or all of these favorable

conditions for the Christian growth of juniors. Others are planning new buildings and changes in organization and time schedule which will make possible such conditions. All churches, however, have it within their power to make changes and adaptations in the direction of these seemingly ideal conditions.

A Place for Learning

The space or rooms set aside for juniors in a local church are not merely places where juniors "meet." They are the environment in which boys and girls make the discoveries, acquire the Christian attitudes, and find opportunities for responding in the ways essential to their Christian growth. Rooms become tools in the planning of thoughtful teachers. Orderliness, beauty, comfort, say to children that the church is a good place to be. Homelikeness, carefully chosen framed pictures, flowers or plants, a friendly arrangement of chairs, extend a welcome. Books, maps, teaching pictures, exhibits, all summon juniors to make discoveries. Chalk board or pads of newsprint suggest that ideas may be shared and plans made together. Tables at which to work, cupboards with an orderly supply of materials, wall space for displaying the work of pupils, stimulate them to express their thinking and feeling about an experience.

Furniture scaled to junior size says to boys and girls that the church cares about their comfort. It often determines the way in which juniors respond to the learning situation. In one church a fifth-grade group used a room which was small for their active ways of learning, but was the only one available. Each Sunday teachers were troubled by the restlessness of the group, by their seeming inability to work toward their purposes for any length of time. When finally junior-sized furniture was placed in the room, the change was astonishing, not alone in the room's appearance but in the working of the group. The teachers found that they, too, were more relaxed when the environment seemed roomier.

Resourceful teachers find ways to create a good learning environment in any kind of church situation. In the one-room church where juniors meet on the front pews, there can always be a small table for a "center of interest," a movable blackboard, and a simple easel for displaying pictures. Hinged shelf tables for work may be attached to the backs of pews and lowered after the session. In the vestibule or at the back of the church panels of wallboard or corkboard allow for display space. Teachers' magazines and manuals give rich guidance at this point.

Something will be planned in the room to call children to quiet thought, to possible worship. Because we know that boys and girls learn best when they have a sense of "oneness" in their experience, we make this center of interest, which may become a center for worship, speak of the unit's meanings and purposes. There will be times when a picture of Jesus will be most meaningful. At other times quite different pictures will be more helpful, and objects will give a silent message. The center for worship may always be considered a piece of visual teaching.

Perhaps juniors are seeking to understand the nature of God. Placed above a picture of children from many lands, these lines will speak of God:

> To Him who made all things that be,
> Yet nothing made the same,
> O lift up heart, O lift up song,
> And glorify His name.[1]

An attractively displayed collection of shells, fruits, or nuts will suggest in still another way the wondrous variety of God's creations. It will make use of a natural interest of juniors.

For juniors we will change the center of interest from week to week. We will avoid the constant use of symbolic objects. A symbol is something we can see used to suggest

[1] Copyright, 1938, by Doris M. Gill and used by her permission.

something we cannot see. Thus candles on either side of a picture of Jesus may possibly mean to the adult who placed them there that Jesus is the Light of the World. They may not mean that to juniors. While juniors are interested in symbols and like to have their meaning interpreted, they still think concretely. But the picture by Elsie Anna Wood of Jesus healing a blind child, placed above a display of a Goodwill bag, the red feather of the Community Chest, the Red Cross, and other objects which are symbols, it is true, but symbols of actual service which boys and girls see rendered in the name or spirit of Jesus, will make a meaningful center for worship.

What Is the Best Grouping?

Classes of juniors can be too large or too small. When the teacher or teachers have difficulty in establishing a warm, friendly feeling with each of the children, when after weeks of being together some seem always on the fringe of the class planning and working, the group is probably too large. When there are not enough boys and girls to stimulate the vigorous flow of ideas, when the group feels limited in its activities because there are not enough to carry out plans they make, then the class is too small. If there are only six or eight pupils in a fourth-grade, a fifth-grade, and a sixth-grade class, better learning will result if these are put together to study, work, and worship as one group. This is especially true if there is a fairly large room where they may spend a full hour. Such a group will use group-graded or cycle-graded lessons.

In a one-grade plan where all boys and girls in Grade 4, for example, meet in their own room during the entire session, with a leading teacher for the unit and a helping teacher for each ten or twelve pupils, a group as large as thirty or thirty-five may be able to do much of their studying and planning, as well as their worshiping and sharing, together. To some teachers twenty seems the ideal size if each child is to participate fully and do good learning. Today some large churches must of necessity plan for one-grade groups numbering as many as eighty pupils. Such churches need to plan toward two or even three Sunday-church-school sessions. Many have found leadership for two sessions and are pleased with the better guidance they can give to juniors. If eighty juniors must meet together at the same hour, the one-grade department with five or six classes and teachers is a necessity. Only thus can the children be known, and helped to become important, contributing members of a true working fellowship.

The classes in a two-grade or three-grade department will vary in size depending upon the space available. If a number of junior classes must meet in one large room, an average attendance of ten or twelve may be all the juniors who can study, think, and work well together without being distracted by what goes on around them. Where classrooms adjoin the large assembly room, somewhat larger groups may be possible, but only if rooms are large enough to permit more boys and girls to learn and work in active ways. Large classes or committees requiring considerable space for their activity may make use of the assembly room or largest classrooms. The use of all rooms should be a flexible matter. No one teacher or grade should ever "own" a room. From year to year, or even unit to unit, the teaching fellowship may determine together how space and other resources can be used for the highest good of all the juniors.

Mixed Classes?

Juniors who are having successful experiences in the public school take a certain pride in their school grade and make their friendships largely within its limits. It seems to form a natural basis or grouping in the church school. From time to time we have a child who has failed to advance with his own age group in the public school. In helping him to find his place at church, the only principle we can follow is the

121

church's concern for the good of persons. He may wish to be in a class with boys and girls his own age, or he may have friends in the school grade and prefer to be a part of that group. His own wishes in the matter are important, for his learning will depend upon the emotions which rule him in the church-school situation. If he is hurt, rebellious, ashamed, he will be learning, of course, but not in ways that will be helpful to his Christian experience.

Among public-school educators there is a growing conviction that the most important learning boys and girls can do is that which enables them to live with all kinds of people in ways that are good. This should be even more a goal of the church, for upon this foundation rests the possibility of true Christian brotherhood. Therefore we will avoid any kind of grouping or grading which sets one child against another or one sex against another. The presence of different kinds of persons provides opportunities for the group to live happily and helpfully with all kinds of people.

It is true that in the junior years boys and girls tend to withdraw into social groupings of their own sex. There are many theories about why this is so, but an obvious reason is the difference in play interests. However, there are boys who enjoy books and games of mental acumen and skill more than they do football. There are girls who wield a powerful baseball bat, who love the active games of "spacemen" and "undercover agents," and are included in clubs made up largely of boys. Wise junior leaders take a middle-of-the-road position. They quietly respect a boy's wish not to sit beside a girl or a girl's uneasiness about having chosen an activity in which only boys are working. They never call attention to it with remarks such as, "Girls don't bite!" or "Those boys need a girl to show them a thing or two!"

When there seems to be open and widespread antagonism between boys and girls, between two boys or two girls, or between two "gangs" of either sex, teachers need to evaluate their own leadership of the group and the adult leadership

122

of these children in groups outside the church. Adults who arouse feelings of hostility and ill will by autocratic discipline, by sarcasm, or by their own hostile attitudes, turn individuals and groups against one another. Such difficulties strike at the very base root of Christianity. Our goal for "increasingly Christlike character" means, quite simply, a growing ability to live with others at home, in the school, in the neighborhood, and at church in the kind, always loving, always forgiving spirit of Jesus. Therefore our class groups ought to provide opportunities for boys and girls to think, work, and grow with other boys and girls. Teachers who feel that they cannot get along with boys or do not know how to talk with girls may grow in their knowledge and understanding of both sexes as they help a class to form some worthy purposes for their learning and work together toward their realization. These teachers will be rewarded by seeing sex antagonism disappear as children become important, contributing members of a group doing worth-while things. When this happens, there is no room and no time for hostility.

Best Use of Time in a Session

Two principles guide us in determining how to use the time available in any kind of session with juniors which the educational program of the church may provide: (1) in so far as possible, boys and girls should feel that all their activities are helping them to move in the same general direction; and (2) groups must have sufficient time to accomplish the worth-while things which they set out to do in a session.

It was these two needs which largely gave rise to the one-grade plan. One grade, meeting for the entire session in a room of its own, may use the time in whatever way will make the richest contribution to the experience of the boys and girls because they do not have to move at a predetermined time into a junior assembly. In some units there may be quite lengthy periods of learning and enjoying hymns. In other units there will be sessions given over to working out plans the group has made, including preparation for a sharing time with parents and friends. The session in which learnings are shared becomes the best review or recall and reuse of experiences which have made up the unit. Often a wise use of time is to rethink all that has taken place in past weeks and under the teacher's guidance to bring these experiences together into moments of worship rich with the sense of God's interest and concern for the boys and girls and what they are doing.

As single grades learn to do good study, planning, working, and worshiping, they find themselves needing more and more time. There are sessions when even two hours are not enough to complete what the group has planned, but juniors leave with a sense of anticipation because they have had sufficient time to become a part of their activities, to give themselves to the experience in active ways.

In every church our planning for juniors should lead to larger and larger blocks of time, but as we work toward this goal, all of us can be learning to use what time we have more wisely. We must discover ways to plan our sessions so that each moment will contribute richly to the growing Christian experience of boys and girls. A rigid time schedule, especially when we try to adhere to it in every session, limits our work and tends toward monotony. Using time flexibly, as is possible in the one-grade plan, can be done within certain limitations by all kinds of junior groups.

In a junior department of any size, as teachers plan together, they may determine how time is to be used within a given unit and how all that is done in each session may contribute to a unified experience. They may decide, for example, that during one unit all classes will come together only once or twice and then for well-defined purposes. In an early session they may wish to share their plans with one another. At the close of the unit they may participate in a carefully planned experience of worship. Or teachers may agree that, when a class needs additional time for work in order to have a feeling of satisfying achievement, they may remain in their classroom and omit the departmental assembly. The superintendent who is a true "helping teacher" will not feel offended when this is done. Rather he will rejoice that boys and girls and their leader have established such strong purposes for their learning that they need and want more time together. He will lead other members of the department to look forward to knowing what this class is doing.

In churches where the church worship service precedes the Sunday-school session, the fifteen or twenty minutes in between, usually given over to "visiting" on the part of adults, may be used by the children's classes for activities related to their units of study. It is possible in this period for a group around the piano to learn new hymns and make other preparations for later worship. Where the children's workers have been able to interpret to adults of the small church the special worship needs of boys and girls, there may be closing moments of worship for the children's classes, even in the front of the one-room church. Boys and girls and their teachers can learn to sing softly without a piano. Adults, continuing their study in the rear pews, can learn to temper their voices or to spend these moments in reading or directed meditation. The small church offers fine opportunities for its members to learn to "live with all kinds of people in ways that are good."

In all kinds of churches additional time may be gained through good use of the twenty minutes or more when children are arriving. When we dispense with the "opening" in a department, juniors and their teachers may set to work at once on class plans. Groups interested enough to come early may have as much additional time as they are willing to make for themselves.

There are good reasons why it is usually wise to plan for worship near the end rather than the beginning of a session. Old and young "need something to worship about." They need experiences which draw them together into a fellowship, and such preparation for worship often comes through the study and work of class groups. When classes are to participate in the worship through the reading of Scripture, choral reading of poems, or some other way of sharing their class learnings, they have an opportunity to prepare for this experience if the study activities come first. Worship helps boys and girls to find meaning and spiritual significance in their church-school experiences. It may be a rich climax to a session. Junior leaders who have tried both types of time schedule will agree that "opening exercises" are well named and seldom merit the term "worship." Boys and girls coming from a variety of home situations, their minds busy with plans for the rest of the day or the movie they saw yesterday, are not "ready" to worship. They are not yet joined in a Christian fellowship of studying, planning, and working, as they will be later in the hour.

Plans for Overcrowded Situations

The use we make of time and the use we make of space offer some possible solutions to the church which is overflowing with boys and girls. Children crowded into inadequate rooms will learn, to be sure. Often, however, they do not learn much that is helpful in their Christian experience. Seldom can they learn as richly and deeply as we desire.

Are there good rooms in your church building which are in use for a scant hour on Sunday morning? Is this true of your own junior assembly room? One of the three grades, working as a single grade, can use this large room, leaving additional classrooms for the other grades. Each grade may have this experience for a quarter or for a unit which seems especially adapted to the large one-grade type of teaching. The juniors using the assembly room will be responsible for arranging it for the closing worship of the department, which seldom lasts longer than twenty minutes.

Churches have successfully housed larger one-grade groups by removing partitions between small classrooms. Not only can more children be accommodated, but the additional room space permits a wider variety of activities and consequently richer learning for all. Churches of the "Akron-plan" type can provide more adequately for the educational program through remodeling. Extending the balcony floor across the large Sunday-school room gives a two-story building. When partitions are taken out between all the small classrooms surrounding the large room on the first floor and balcony, it is possible to make good-sized rooms.

The small church may have church homes nearby where classes of youth and adults could hold their Sunday-morning sessions, thereby leaving additional rooms in the church building for children. In some communities school buildings or large halls are available. Every church needs to think its way out of an overcrowded situation. The friendliness of reasonably small groups; a pleasant, comfortable environment; and the opportunity to participate in worth-while activities are all essential to the Christian growth of children. Churches dare not relinquish these, even though the very large child population of the present day makes it difficult to maintain them.

Rearrangement of the Sunday-morning schedule has helped many churches to do better educational work. A double session of the church school for children is possible and feasible in most situations. Some congregations are holding two services of worship, with church-school classes for youth and adults between the two services. During the first service of worship juniors may use not only their own rooms but those later occupied by youth and adult classes. While young people and adults are in church-school groups, junior boys and girls may have fellowship, sharing, and worship experiences in the sanctuary. Children younger than third grade will do their best learning by spending the two hours in their own rooms in a carefully planned and guided expanded session.

If the juniors are to be in the sanctuary for most of one

hour, their teachers must make the preceding class sessions times of active learning, with a minimum of sitting and listening. The sanctuary service must be planned for maximum participation on the part of the children with opportunities to share from their graded-lesson experiences and materials. It should not attempt to duplicate the general order of worship for adult services. Further suggestions for the expanded or additional session of juniors are given in the next chapter.

The church which is really concerned that its people shall progress toward the goals of Christian education will not limit learning to Sunday morning. It will give ever-increasing thought to the whole educational program. For its work it will consider the possibilities of after-school hours, of the longer Sunday-morning session, of Sunday afternoon, weekday, or vacation time, of the Saturdays which the church has relinquished without a struggle to the neighborhood movie house.

CHAPTER TEN

What Is an Effective Church Program for Juniors?

To BE EFFECTIVE, the church program for juniors must provide ample opportunities for these boys and girls to have the experiences and participate in the activities through which they may grow in Christian knowledge, attitudes, and living. They are growing and changing through everything that happens to them in each hour of each day. We would wish that all these experiences might take place under Christian guidance or be interpreted by Christian parents and friends in the ways which would contribute most to Christian growth. While it is not possible so to guide the daily and hourly growth of every child, it is possible for the church to plan rich, well-rounded experiences during the hours that junior boys and girls spend within the church fellowship.

What Kinds of Activities?

Juniors must grow in knowledge and conduct, and in devotional practices which will nurture their faith now and in the years ahead. They must grow into the fellowship of Christians in the local church and in the world Church. They must grow in Christian concern for others everywhere.

Such growth takes place as boys and girls participate in ways of learning which make full use of their interests and abilities. They grow as they are challenged to discover and think, as they use and share what they have discovered. They grow through every activity which makes their Christian learning important and worth while to them, and valued by persons they love and admire. They grow through the on-

going experiences which develop over a period of time and through the smaller activities which contribute to these larger experiences.

For You to Do

As you read the following list, write "much," "some," "little," or "none" beside each kind of activity to indicate how much opportunity boys and girls of your church have to participate in this way of learning for Christian living. Think of your entire church program for juniors, not merely of the Sunday-morning session.

Reading to make discoveries in the Bible, in their study books, in resource materials, in background storybooks, in denominational story papers

Participating in guided discussion to discover meanings in words, ideas, Bible passages, hymns

Explaining to others the meanings they have found

Listening to and enjoying stories

Listening to talking pictures, or movies

Listening to hymns and other music

Discovering information, stories, messages, in flat pictures or in projected pictures

Studying maps for information

Taking trips to find out about other people, places, ways of worshiping, how the church serves others

Dramatizing everyday experiences to show what they consider Christian choices

Dramatizing a problem, putting themselves in the place of other persons to see how they feel about a situation and how it might be solved in a Christian way

Planning through guided discussion how to use discoveries, how to share them with others

Retelling and choosing stories for dramatization

Choosing Bible passages, hymns, poems to learn

Dramatizing and/or illustrating hymns, Scripture, poems, stories

130

Memorizing

Choral reading

Singing hymns meaningfully and joyfully

Making maps to record discoveries

Making and using charts as reminders, records, for memorizing

Making a time line

Making research cards

Making class record books, picture books for gifts, storybooks or picture books to add to class library

Writing brief stories, plays, prayers, litanies, poems, psalms, letters, reports, items for church newspaper

Reporting orally discoveries they have made

Sharing discoveries through art activities—drawing or painting pictures, posters, friezes, murals, movies on wooden rollers; making peep shows, dioramas, slides for projecting

Planning programs to share discoveries in a unit

Planning and preparing centers for worship

Selecting and organizing materials for worship

Worshiping informally in class sessions

Worshiping with other junior groups

Worshiping at home with the family

Worshiping as individuals at home

Worshiping in the church service of worship

Worshiping in the outdoors

Praying silently, as teacher guides their thinking

Praying their own thoughts aloud in the group

Reading prayers, choosing some to learn

Using hymns as prayers

Getting acquainted with the minister, with other church officers and leaders

Giving money for local church projects

Helping to care for and beautify the church property

Taking care of junior rooms, equipment, supplies

Making equipment or useful gifts for younger groups

Taking part in whole-church activities, such as a school of missions, a special Christmas giving project, family-fellowship times

Planning fun and fellowship for own group; for others

Engaging in group living under Christian guidance, at home, in clubs, classwork, game periods, camping experiences

Giving money to help share the gospel with others

Making and sending gifts to mission stations, settlement houses, homes for aged and children

Visiting other churches, denominations, faiths

Making friendships with Christians of other lands

For You to Decide

Which of the above activities could be used satisfactorily in each of the following kinds of sessions for juniors?

Sunday-Morning Sessions of the Church School

This partial list of activities clearly indicates that one hour on Sunday morning is not enough time for Christian teaching. One hour is even less adequate when it is divided between two programs and two leaders, as in a half-hour of "worship service" under a junior superintendent and a half-hour of "class period" for which the class teacher is responsible.

Thus a first step toward a more effective program for juniors may be to find the space for larger groups, possibly single grades, or in smaller churches for the twenty or thirty boys and girls of junior age, to study, work, and worship for a full hour or more in their own room, under one leadership.

As churches grow concerned for the effectiveness of their educational work with all ages, including juniors, they will consider ways to rearrange the morning schedule so that one-and-a-quarter or one-and-a-half hours are available for church school. This longer church-school hour is especially important in communities where it is the established practice of families to attend together the church service of worship. These churches may not favor the expanded session described below or the additional session held during the hour of church-worship service. However, they may provide one and a half hours for church-school experiences. The longer period, when it is well planned, need not be fatiguing to children. Indeed, they will find the wider variety of active ways to learn more restful and inviting than a shorter session in which they do much sitting.

An increasing number of churches have an expanded Sunday-morning session. Boys and girls work and study, worship and serve, in an informal atmosphere of Christian fellowship for two or more hours. Regular church-school materials contain additional content and suggestions for the longer session. The same staff of teachers works throughout the morning. Continuity of leadership and of program makes possible the "unified experience" necessary for the best learning.

Planning for the expanded session is rather like planning for a morning of vacation school. Its values, too, are similar. There is time to know boys and girls well, to think through problems, to undertake and carry to successful completion large plans which the group makes, to provide a rich variety of learning experiences, and to worship at times when the group seems most ready.

A church may adopt this program when teachers have learned to use their materials so well that they feel a need and a desire for more time. The first step toward an expanded session is the enlistment and development of alert, able, enthusiastic teachers who are constantly growing in interest in their work and concern for their children. To maintain adequate leadership is a continuing problem, however. More and more workers must be fed into the teaching program and a strong fellowship developed among them. They must have frequent opportunities to meet and evaluate

133

the effectiveness of their work, to rejoice together in their successes, and to find good ways of solving problems. The church family, and the church commission on education in particular, need to give recognition and appreciation to persons who through the expanded session make a truly large contribution to the Christian growth of boys and girls.

Ways must be found to keep a few persons from bearing too heavy responsibilities. Two or three teachers working with one group of boys and girls may take turns serving as the leading teacher, each being responsible for one unit, the others acting as helping teachers. Some churches maintain the expanded session only through the months when attendance is most regular. The remainder of the year families attend the church service of worship, and a shorter church-school session is held. Other teachers may then relieve the expanded session staff. Each church must work out its own solution to the problem of leadership, but the expanded session will die if teachers feel unable to handle the work and are not happy with the results.

To secure the continuing co-operation of parents is a second problem of the expanded session. If most fathers and mothers attend both the morning worship and a church-school class, there is little difficulty. However, where families are faithful only to the morning worship or to the church school, teachers face the discouraging situation of many children leaving at the end of the first hour or arriving when the session is half over. A church should do careful preparatory planning with parents before undertaking an expanded church-school session. It must continue to educate families, both new and old.

Additional Sessions

Additional sessions are any or all the ways in which a church provides added time for the Christian nurture of its boys and girls. They should be planned by all the leaders of juniors for all the juniors and should not be considered separate organizations, with independent leadership or membership. They have added importance in these days, especially for churches which find their buildings overflowing with children on Sunday morning and consequently hindered in doing effective work at that time. Groups of children meeting on weekdays or at hours on Sunday other than during the morning church-school session can enjoy ample space and often periods of time more adequate for working out their plans.

The Sunday morning additional session. In many churches children meet during the adult worship service on Sunday morning in a session which is frequently called "junior church." The effectiveness of this "additional session," as it should be called, can be increased if the age range is limited to Grades 3 or 4 through 5 or 6, depending upon whether the two-grade or three-grade department operates in the church school. Children younger than this need their own kind of session in their own church-school room, planned by their own leaders.

The Sunday-morning additional session for juniors should be planned by all junior workers, and they may take turns, each being responsible for leadership of a unit. It should not attempt to duplicate the adult order of worship, with its high point a so-called "children's sermon." Too many of these are moralizing talks or "object lessons" which disregard the known inability of juniors to see relationships between the tangible and intangible. There are far better ways for boys and girls to learn than by being "preached at" or "talked to." Many "junior-church" sessions are a serious waste of the church's teaching opportunity. Using this additional time in the following ways will contribute more to the Christian growing of boys and girls:

1. *To supplement the limited time of the church-school session.* The Sunday-morning additional session for juniors will differ from the expanded session in that pupils from all junior grades may meet together, although their church-school experience is closely graded. They may meet in a different room and with different leadership than that of the

church-school session. Thus there will not be the unity which is so valuable in the expanded session. However, in churches where teachers are not yet ready to give a full morning to the work, and where not all boys and girls are encouraged by parents to remain throughout the longer period, the additional session may be preferable. Leaders may develop the session around the experiences of the juniors' graded lessons and use additional materials for which there is not time in church-school classes or departmental assemblies. This, for example, may be the ideal time for the projected visual resources suggested in a unit, a time when the best room for this purpose can be used by the juniors. If the film or filmstrip is to be effective in the experiences of a unit, it must be shown under the direction of a junior teacher who knows the purpose for using it and how to help the boys and girls get the greatest good from it.

The time may be used for the thorough learning and for the enjoying of devotional materials from the church-school units. An unhurried hymn interpretation, with the story of its writing, with discussion of meaning, pictures or slides to illustrate it, and ample time to learn and enjoy the melody, will be a worthy use of this hour while adults are worshiping in the sanctuary. A Psalm may be enjoyed and made into a choral reading.

As the juniors are studying units about the church, they may study the order of worship in the adult service and make plans to attend such a service. They may learn to sing one of the hymns and to read the responsive reading which the minister plans to use when they are present.

One grade or class may report on an experience in the unit such as a trip made to a settlement house or to a home for aged persons or homeless children. With the report may be used pictures of Jesus healing and helping, stories told or read from the Bible to interpret these pictures, and a meaningful hymn, such as "O Brother Man, Fold to Thy Heart Thy Brother."

2. *As "extra sessions."* At certain periods of the year this time may be used for the kinds of extra sessions suggested in the church-school lesson materials, for rehearsing a play, as a "Christmas workshop," to get ready for Mother's Day.

3. *For missionary education.* In addition to the time spent in the study of missionary units in the Sunday-church-school curriculum, additional sessions should be available for study of the missionary units on the emphasis for the year.

Some denominations regularly offer such units in their teachers' magazine under a title such as "Additional Sessions for Juniors."

The hour while adults are worshiping should contribute meaningfully to the experiences of junior boys and girls. It should offer opportunities for Christian growing needed by juniors, as listed earlier in this chapter.

Sessions Outside Sunday Morning

Additional sessions held on Sunday afternoon or evening, or at a period during the week, may do any or all of the things suggested for the Sunday-morning additional session. There are still other opportunities which boys and girls may enjoy, whether they meet only occasionally, or weekly or monthly throughout the year, or in several consecutive weekly sessions once or twice a year.

Opportunities for *supervised play* will help juniors to grow in Christian relationships with others. All juniors should have *occasional times of fun and fellowship* and wholesome play with their adult leaders in the church. Such experiences lead to increased interest and co-operation.

The *church-membership class* for older juniors, whether it is led by the minister or by some other person, is one kind of additional session. Denominations provide special courses of study for juniors preparing to join the church. Just as in any other kind of learning experience, boys and girls need leaders who will help them to find purposes which are worth while to them, who will guide them in actively seeking information and doing the interesting things through which they learn best. "Telling" and "question-and-answer" teaching are no more effective in the church-membership class than in any other phase of a junior's Christian growing.

In a *junior choir* the boys and girls participating in the experience should be the first concern of the leader. What opportunities for Christian growing do these choir sessions offer to juniors? What kind of hymns, responses, and simple anthems will be meaningful to the boys and girls, and can be sung by them with joyousness? How may their choir experience enrich worship in the church-school sessions? The stories of hymns and their writers, the enjoyment of recordings, the discussion of experiences suggested by the music and the words, pictures, slides, films, may all contribute from time to time to the richness of experience which helps boys and girls to sing gladly and with growing religious insight.

The choir leader who plans thus finds that he cannot hope to prepare juniors to sing in Sunday services each week. The pressure of such a schedule makes choir rehearsals times of drill and often of fatigue and frustration for both children and leader. To provide anthems for the adult service of worship is not the purpose of the junior choir.

At certain seasons, on certain occasions, these boys and girls may contribute to congregational worship out of their own rich enjoyment of music. They need this incentive and purpose for their choir work. The leader with a true feeling for music and an understanding of what it can mean in the Christian experience of boys and girls will use this children's choir in special, meaningful ways. Coming quietly down the aisle at a Christmas vesper, looking with anticipation at the manger scene in the front of the church, and pausing before it to sing softly and beautifully "Come Softly, Tread Gently" [1] is a finer experience for juniors than to stand

[1] From *Fifty Christmas Carols of All Nations;* Willis Music Co.

resplendent in the choir pews singing with strain and difficulty a two- or three-part arrangement of an anthem which they do not understand, cannot sing well, and consequently do not enjoy. Many leaders of junior choirs make excellent use of music found in the church-school materials for juniors or in the hymnals recommended for this age group.

Vacation Church School

The vacation church school, of two to six weeks, with two- to three-hour sessions each day, is one of the year's richest learning opportunities for juniors and for their teachers. A high level of interest can be maintained because the boys and girls come to the church each day. There is ample time in a session for the group to plan and work, study and worship and play together, to engage in all the kinds of experience through which an area of the Christian faith may become truly meaningful.

Many courses of study are available for the special use of juniors in vacation school, and many are prepared cooperatively by the denominations. Here again, for the reasons given in Chapter Four, choices should be made from the recommended curriculum of the denomination.

Under an experienced supervisor the vacation school may become one of the finest teacher-training opportunities the church can provide. Teachers are usually working under conditions far more ideal than those which prevail on Sunday mornings. There is more time. The entire church building is at the disposal of the children. All kinds of activities are possible. Usually the juniors who choose to attend are those most eager and ready to learn. A good supervisor will encourage workers to try out new ways of guiding juniors, to use informal procedures, to plan *with* boys and girls rather than *for* them, to carry over some of the good methods and good results of vacation school into all teaching sessions with juniors throughout the year, including those of Sunday morning.

Church Camping With Juniors

Leisurely days of camp life, under the guidance of well-trained, mature, Christian leaders, help juniors to discover in the outdoors evidences of God's planning. They have time to think deeply about the Christian meaning of life and of man's part and place in God's universe. They participate fully in group living, with its attendant problems and troubles, and learn to meet these in Christian ways. They grow in Christian concern for their fellows.

The church must not bring together masses of children, nor subject them to the undue stimulation of a crowded schedule. Highest values lie in a small camp enrolling not more than fifty or sixty juniors. These fifty or sixty will live in small groups of four to six boys or girls with an adult leader. Two such groups join to engage in daytime activities. If the leaders can be church friends, persons to whom boys and girls look for guidance throughout the year, the values of camping are multiplied. Such persons must have deep convictions about the Christian faith and concern for the religious growing of children. They must know and like juniors. They must be experienced in outdoor living or be willing to learn the skills needed.

Church commissions on education who feel that their people are ready to venture into this kind of vacation teaching opportunity will investigate the possibilities of (1) resident camping where boys and girls and their mature leaders carry on all the activities of life in the outdoors during the day and spend the nights together in the camp; (2) a variation of this where the camp site is on a farm, and farm duties and activities are a part of the program; and (3) day camping in which juniors and their leaders live together outdoors during the day, but spend the nights in their homes.

Planning for a church camp and the training of leaders is a large and important undertaking, one which requires many months of preparation. Denominations and the Na-

140

tional Council of Churches provide excellent guidance materials for use in camping with juniors.

The Christian Growth of the Whole Child

Some churches provide the kinds of sessions described above and still do not do an effective piece of Christian teaching. Organizations and leaders, instead of being united within the junior department of the church school, compete for the interest and time of juniors. They need to join forces for the most effective Christian guidance of this age group.

A unit, we have said, is a group of carefully chosen, carefully guided experiences through which purposes of the unit may be realized. Thus at any given period of the church year all junior activities should lead toward realization of one set of purposes. The planning chart suggested on page 107 will show the general area in which all members of the junior department are likely to be working. Its listing of "Things the Juniors Will Be Doing" may be even fuller and richer if guidance for these may be divided among the Sunday-morning sessions, weekday additional sessions, choir, church-membership class, a craft and related play group, and so on.

For You to Do

1. Suggest activities for each kind of junior session described above when these boys and girls are looking toward the Easter season or when they are engaged in this year's mission-study units.

2. Complete the following sentences:

"The best ways for my church to strengthen its work with juniors would be to . . . ."

"We could begin now to . . . ."

"I will try to awaken interest in improving our church program for juniors by . . . ."

141

CHAPTER ELEVEN

Enlisting Parents as Fellow Teachers of Religion

JUNIOR BOYS AND GIRLS spend comparatively few hours in the church or under the guidance of church leaders. Leaders in Christian education are increasingly convinced that the finest learning experiences the church can plan are not enough to develop in boys and girls sturdy Christian convictions and consistent Christian practices, since children are constantly learning in all the hours they spend away from the supervision of the church. They learn to live religiously or irreligiously, depending upon the kind of guidance they have, upon the way that adults help them to interpret and react to the situations of which they are a part.

More and more we are looking to the home as the real school of Christian living, and to parents as the teachers who most consistently influence boys and girls for good or ill. Some denominations have developed detailed plans whereby the local church can vastly increase the effectiveness of its curriculum by helping parents to do their share of Christian teaching. Others are experimenting with such a program. All recognize that this is a large undertaking, one which needs and deserves the best in leadership, as well as steady, year-in-year-out cultivation. The church with an adequate staff of trained, full-time workers can give itself to this work in a more organized, persistent, and effectual way than can the great majority of churches which are staffed by volunteers. However, in any situation the program is ultimately one of winning individual homes and individual parents to assume responsibility for their task of Christian teaching, of helping each parent to grow in Christian knowledge and devotion, and learn how to guide his children in Christian living. Thus the smaller church may have a certain advantage in developing the personal relationship between homes and the church, between parents and church-school teachers.

The superintendent and teachers of a junior department may work with parents of their boys and girls when the church as a whole has not caught a vision of this opportunity. Even one interested junior teacher may enlist an increasing number of parents as his fellow teachers at home. In principle the following suggestions are equally applicable to a church-wide, a junior-department, or a junior-class plan for guiding parents to help their children grow as Christian persons.

Fellow Teachers Must Be Friends

A genuine liking for every junior, a warm-hearted concern for each member of his family, opens the door to friendship with his parents. To grow, this relationship must rest upon respect for one another and faith in good intentions. Through our own experiences as sons and daughters and parents, we can believe that fathers and mothers love their children and want the best for them. Certainly there will be few exceptions among parents who enroll their boys and girls in the church school. Some, to be sure, will not find the church significant to them as adults. Some will have a superficial view of what constitutes the "best" for boys and girls. These merely represent ways in which parents need to grow. Such growth is almost inevitable if the church can win them to help in the Christian learning of their children. Meanwhile, even with those who are at present unwilling to help, a staunch faith in the essential goodness of parents makes it possible for friendship between home and church, between parent and teacher, to grow and strengthen.

As friendship grows, the teacher may discover important values in the family life of boys and girls. He may be astonished and rewarded for his faith in fathers and mothers. He will learn special ways to enlist individual parents as his fellow Christian teachers. He will become a trusted friend because he cares about and appreciates a child. Perhaps he can help parents to a better understanding and fuller enjoyment of their own junior.

Good Things Happen to Children at Church

Our churches are full of adults who do not expect children to learn much of anything in the church school. This attitude is reflected in the attendance of boys and girls who come when it is convenient. It is sometimes apparent in church boards. Thirty minutes, they may say, is "enough time for what a Sunday-school class does." The junior department does not need a copy of the Revised Standard Version of the Bible for each child, "just to look up a few verses." These persons simply do not expect any real teaching or learning to take place.

Hence to many fathers and mothers it is both astonishing and gratifying to find that some persons take their Sunday-school teaching seriously. They marvel that certain teachers are willing to hold additional sessions, to plan for trips, to call in the homes. They react with warm appreciation to the teacher who shares with them some incident about their child's church-school experience. Such opportunities present themselves in the grocery store, on the bus, at church meetings or social gatherings. Just as it is one responsibility of the public-school teacher to help make the community aware of the value of the school, so it is a responsibility of the church-school teacher to help parents know what is going on there.

A letter to all parents at the beginning of the year may establish the teacher's purpose to help boys and girls learn and grow. It makes clear that the teacher thinks Christian teaching is important and is willing to give his time and effort.

Dear Mr. and Mrs. ——— :

In our church-school class John is beginning a study called "Understanding the Early Old Testament." It reviews stories of familiar Old Testament leaders to help the boys and girls discover how these persons grew in their understanding of God. We hope to help our juniors clear up their own thinking about what God is like. I could be more helpful to John if you would let me know by telephone or note any confused ideas he may have about God or any puzzling problems about what God does or does not do in the world.

John will bring his study book home next Sunday. Will you read pages ——— with him? Perhaps you will find some ideas worth discussing in the family. From time to time I will send a post card asking you to help John in certain other ways. Our class session is so short and it is so long between Sundays that we need John's father and mother to be his special "helping teachers" at home.

To be sure, letters and cards to parents take time, but they express our sincere intentions as teachers. The person who is very busy or who has a large class may look for a helper who will act as corresponding secretary. Often there are people in the church who cannot teach, but do own a typewriter and have time to write notes or post cards.

We Will Learn as We Teach

Many parents of our boys and girls believe that Christian teaching is important. They would like to do more of it at home if they knew how. Those of us who have had no special training in the teaching of religion know how much there is to be learned and how inadequate an adult can feel about his own background of religious knowledge and experience. Even the Old Testament stories of our childhood may be hazy

145

in detail. Few adults really know how the Bible came into being or have the necessary background for interpreting the Bible accurately. Many have done little growing in religious concepts since childhood. Some have grown up in an atmosphere of reticence about religion and find it most difficult to speak aloud their religious beliefs, feelings, or needs.

For these reasons our approach to parents will be that all of us—teachers and parents—may *learn with our juniors.* The denominational junior courses of study are rich in information about the Bible and the most helpful ways to interpret and use it in our own day, about the Bible land and Bible times, about the significance of Jesus' life as well as its facts, about what it means to be a Christian and how the Christian serves the world through his church. Teachers of juniors often speak of how much they have learned as they prepare to teach from week to week.

If we are careful not to overwhelm parents with all that needs to be learned and taught, if we can lead them one step at a time and help them to feel satisfaction in their own discoveries about religion, as well as in their experiences of guiding their children, then we shall gradually help them to become effective Christian teachers.

Specific Guidance to Parents

We must begin by being very definite in our requests, by suggesting certain pages in the pupil's book to study with the junior in the home, a Bible passage to read together and perhaps to memorize, a book from the church library or the public library to enjoy together, one kind of news item to watch for and bring to church school, a subject for the family to discuss and about which the junior may report in class his family's opinions and conclusions.

The denominational curriculum for juniors guides us at this point. The teacher's helps or manual carry suggestions for each unit and sometimes session by session of activities to be carried out in the family. Some of these are reading and study. Some are for family devotional periods. Some are activities within the community or ways of serving others. The teacher's job is to find the most effective ways of bringing these to the attention of families and of creating a desire on the part of juniors and their parents to share in these activities at home.

As fathers and mothers search their own Christian experience and knowledge in order to think with their children, they will develop a sense of need at many points and begin to ask for help. Teachers may guide as far as they are able, through sharing some of the background materials in their teachers' manuals, through making available the resource books listed for the help of teachers, through planning discussion meetings led by someone more informed than they are or by someone who is skilled in guiding the thinking of persons about what constitutes worthy Christian living. Many pastors welcome opportunities to be of help when teachers and parents are searching for religious knowledge and Christian insight. Some churches have full-time professional leadership in Christian education. In other churches teachers and parents may have to read and study independently. As they dig out their own information, search for points of view which clarify their thinking and fit into their own religious experience, and share with each other what they find useful, they will learn more than those who simply call upon a professional Christian worker to tell them what they need to know or believe. The superintendent of the children's division, or of the junior department, or one junior teacher in a small church may prepare himself to lead the study of the parent-teacher group.

There are good sources of help for guiding parents who are willing to be our fellow teachers of juniors. Some denominations provide a magazine for parents dealing with many aspects of Christian home life. Its special study units give guidance in beliefs and backgrounds which help parents to increase their knowledge and examine and strengthen their own faith. Some of these units are closely related to experiences juniors boys and girls are having in the church school.

So, too, are units in the denominational curriculum for adult classes. Junior leaders should be familiar with these and ready to bring them to the attention of parents. In many communities leadership-education schools or classes offer courses which will help parents to become informed and effective home teachers.

For You to Do

In your junior course of study find all the suggestions for contacting parents and enlisting them to help their children learn at home during the unit. What specific assignments for home study are given? If there are no such suggestions, make your own plans for ways that parents may work with you.

Parents, Children, and Teachers Meet Together

It is important to plan with parents rather than for them. Their interest and their learning from the experience will be in direct proportion to their participation. While it is thoroughly desirable to hold a planning meeting with fathers and mothers at the beginning of the school year, if this is a first attempt, it may be wiser to delay it until the close of the juniors' first unit of study. By this time the teacher of a class or those in a department may have built up a nucleus of friendly, interested, appreciative parents who will help to make the meeting successful both in attendance and in program. By this time from their church-school experience the boys and girls will have something worth sharing with their families.

The purpose of the meeting will be threefold: to create the start of a fellowship feeling among all who are concerned for the Christian education of junior boys and girls, to help parents discover through the work of the juniors in the unit just completed that good things do take place in the church school, and to encourage fathers and mothers to believe that they can help at home with the Christian teaching of their children.

148

These purposes are so important that the juniors may well use time in a Sunday-morning session to help plan for such a meeting. Some of the parents who are already interested may be present, too. When the time and place for the meeting have been decided by the group, other plans will probably require three committees: (1) invitations and getting-acquainted plans; (2) program, much of which will be the sharing of work and learning from the unit now being completed by the boys and girls; and (3) refreshments, for food is a "must" when juniors meet socially.

The adults who are helping may give special thought to certain families who are not active in the church and may not come to the meeting, even at the urging of their own child. A call in such homes with an offer of transportation may finally bring results, even though it proves unsuccessful this first time. Especially friendly parents may sponsor those who are new and be personally responsible for helping them to get acquainted and feel comfortable in the group.

The program through which the boys and girls share what they have learned as they worked in the unit will be doubly valuable if parents are at least partially informed about the study from having read the pupil's book or having helped their own junior in ways requested by the teacher. Sometimes the teacher or teachers may plan a special way of adding still more to the experiences of the unit for both juniors and parents.

On one such occasion as children were concluding the unit "The Homeland of Jesus," the rabbi whose temple they had visited was a "surprise guest." With the parents he enjoyed the sharing program of the juniors. He then spoke appreciatively of this church's efforts to help its people learn more about the roots of their religion, which lay in the Hebrew faith. He offered to try to answer any questions parents or children might have about his way of worshiping God. His reply to a little girl who asked why he did not read the New Testament astonished many. "I read it often," he said, "sometimes every day. But in my own home, not to my people in the temple." The opportunity to know the rabbi as a cultured, friendly, gracious person, one acquainted with the Christian faith and respectful of it, was of great value to parents, teachers, and children.

Missionary units afford similar opportunities in communities where there are persons from other lands. However, junior leaders need to know something of these persons before they are invited to speak to boys and girls and parents. Some will contribute much to the purposes of a unit. Others will not.

To close the sharing time of a unit on the "Teachings of Jesus," the teachers planned to use John Charles Thomas' beautiful recording of "The Lord's Prayer." The lights were dimmed and a spotlight thrown upon a picture of Jesus teaching his disciples. Listening to the recording helped many in the group to worship.

Look Ahead to the Coming Unit

Some special plan of this kind may introduce parents and juniors to the next unit and help them begin their learning even before the first Sunday session of its use. As the boys and girls start a study of the life of Jesus, one of the films from the series called "Two Thousand Years Ago" will help them, their parents, and their teachers to visualize the setting of Jesus' life and ministry.

If a trip is one of the important activities of the new unit, juniors and adults may begin to make plans for it, to decide upon a time when the family can enjoy it together. All will make note of any preparatory study which will help them to understand what they will see and so to learn more richly from the experience. Here, again, some projected visual materials might be used, such as slides or filmstrip of the activities in an institutional church or in a settlement house.

While the boys and girls engage in another activity, a teacher may share with parents some of the background information for the new unit, its point of view, perhaps, or the interpretation of key Bible passages. Parents may receive typed lists of ways that they can help with the experiences of this unit. The resource books suggested for teachers and for boys and girls may be available, to be borrowed by interested parents.

Whatever takes place in this first meeting should help parents to feel that "this is something worth while that all of us are doing together," not that the church "is trying to tell us what to do." They should go away feeling that they *want* to help their boys and girls keep learning and growing, and that they can. Nothing should be purposely said or done to make them feel inadequate or that they have failed in the past. Such feelings will come as parents get into the job of teaching religion at home. However, when others arouse in us a sense of inadequacy for a new task, we seldom undertake it.

Other Kinds of Help from Parents

As parents become increasingly interested in the church experiences of their juniors, they may be encouraged to take a larger and larger share in planning for the class or department. Some will prove valuable helping teachers in the class sessions of a unit. "Class parents," like the P.T.A. homeroom mothers in public school, may serve for a quarter. They may help with telephoning, publicity, and contacting parents of new pupils. Helpers for additional sessions, for vacation school, and counselors for a church camp may be enlisted from an active and interested parents-of-juniors group. As teachers and parents become better acquainted, ways will be found to help each father and mother contribute in his own best way to the learning experiences of his child at church as well as at home.

Problems will arise in the junior department about which "we need your advice as parents." If tardiness is one, a small committee of parents may be asked to attend the junior sessions for a month, inquire into the causes and analyze the effect of this condition upon the learning of the department. They may then present a report and some constructive plan of action to the teacher-parent group when next it meets.

If more time for teaching is needed on Sunday morning, a committee of parents and teachers may visit other churches and bring back reports of what is being done elsewhere. They may present this need to the church board if a change of Sunday-morning schedule seems to be the answer. The church commission on education which feels that its teaching staff is ready to undertake an expanded session will do well to make committees of parents responsible for publicizing and "selling" the plan to all church families.

Interested parents will be concerned that the the juniors have all necessary supplies and equipment for good learning, including Bibles, hymnals, blackboards, mounting boards, visual aids, comfortable furniture, and attractive rooms. However, the need for such things must be presented by teachers who take their work seriously, who will make use of them for more effective teaching of boys and girls.

Parents who know from the experiences of their own families that good things are happening in the educational work of the church can help to make the whole church fellowship aware of this and proud that theirs is becoming more and more a teaching church.

A Class or Department of "Church Homes"

The children who come to us from "unchurched homes" need a special measure of our friendship, understanding, and active goodwill. Some parents require long cultivation before they begin to take an interest in the church or in what the church is doing with their boys and girls. Few, however, are untouched by kindness to their children and genuine interest in them. The teacher who sees that no junior is left out of class activities simply because his parents will not be present,

152

the teacher who calls for a child and brings him home from a learning excursion or social occasion, is actually witnessing for the Christian faith. He is helping a family indifferent to Christianity to discover through their own experience that the Christian person and the Christian Church value every child.

Sometimes we help by recognizing and acknowledging that persons can and do have experiences which create feelings of hostility to religion. "Of course you do not want Peggy to suffer as you did because someone made you so afraid of God. Let me bring you some of our teaching materials. You read them and decide for yourself how Peggy will learn to feel about God from her experiences in our church school."

To serve one of these families in a time of crisis or tragedy is the opportunity and privilege of the minister and the church-school teacher who have been friends in happier days. Christian love at times like these has led many parents to the realization that they need the church.

Sometimes we label a home "unchurched" without justification. "In our twelve years of living in this community," one father said, "no one from the church has ever called on us before." Yet his children were more or less regular attendants of the church school. Being "wanted" brought this family into the church fellowship as faithful, interested, working members.

Every junior worker will desire that each child he teaches shall be guided by parents who are strongly influenced by the church. A class or department of "church homes" will be his goal, a goal worthy of his time and best efforts. Long ago in Palestine, Jesus felt compassion for every person who did not know God the Father and did not live secure in his love. Our unflagging helpfulness and friendliness will speak to many parents of God's bountiful love available to them.

CHAPTER TWELVE

Evaluating Our Work
With Juniors

ARE THE BOYS AND GIRLS of the church growing in the Christian faith? How are we to know?

Are we who guide juniors growing with them in the faith? Are we learning to live with them lovingly and to teach them skillfully? How may we determine our strengths and our weaknesses as teachers?

Growth is so gradual, so quiet, so constant, that much of the time we are unaware of it. Suddenly a boy's wrist bones show below the sleeves of his jackets or a girl grown tall looks levelly into our eyes. In the same sudden ways we become aware of Christian growth. These moments of awareness must be treasured and recorded, for they indicate the progress our boys and girls are making in the Christian life.

Indications of Growth

One Sunday as Mike expressed indignation over something heard on the radio, his teacher knew that he had grown in Christian attitudes.

Mickey had been silent during a lively discussion of the commandments. Two Sundays later another child accidentally stepped on his map. Swiftly, angrily, Mickey swore. With stricken eyes he looked at the teacher and muttered, "I didn't mean to say that!"

"I know you didn't mean to, Mickey," she said. "It's not an easy habit to break. Thinking about how good God is, how great he is, and the loving kindness which we see all about us keeps us from using his name thoughtlessly and care-

154

lessly. When you first wake up each morning, will you try to repeat and think about the hymn we often sing,

> There's a wideness in God's mercy,
> Like the wideness of the sea?"

Mickey nodded silently. A few moments later the teacher saw that he was copying the hymn on a filing card.

A parent reported to the minister that through his experiences in the church-membership class a junior boy's prayers had changed. Instead of repeating phrases he had used for years, he now expressed gratitude for the Christian fellowship and asked that he himself and the Christian Church might help all men everywhere to know and serve God. The minister suggested that the family read some thrilling missionary adventures and think together about the relation of one's praying to one's giving.

In the same group where one girl wrote of Jesus:

> He lived like God
> For men to see,

another child painted her understanding of what Jesus meant to the people who knew him in Palestine. In drab shades she pictured a narrow street between tall buildings. A few dark figures huddled against the buildings, but through the street walked Jesus in robes of glistening white. "Jesus loved the poor people," she said, "and they knew it."

One class had an unusually happy experience in gathering Christmas gifts for a mountain school. When the next letter from their church missionary in Brazil was read to the department, one junior protested, "But he didn't tell us anything we could send him. What does he need?"

"Yes, how can we help him?" the children chorused and composed a letter asking what useful gifts they might send to the little church in Brazil.

155

One day we may observe that our juniors now need little help in using the Bible. They handle it as a book familiar and valued. Suddenly we are aware that the boys and girls participate gladly and wholeheartedly in worship, that they enjoy planning and preparing for it.

As the year goes on, we realize that our juniors are friendlier and kinder, that they defer courteously to wishes of the majority, that certain ones have ceased to goad each other or to vie for attention.

In discussion we are astonished at intelligent questions, good thinking, flashes of insight. We share the wonder of those long-ago teachers who talked with a young boy in the Temple at Jerusalem; for our juniors, too, are growing "in wisdom and in stature, and in favor with God and man."

Records Worth Keeping

The most important records we can keep are such evidences that our juniors are growing in the Christian faith and as helpful members of the Christian fellowship.

When junior teachers meet to plan for coming units, they will be heartened and their fellowship strengthened if they share with one another from the unit or units now nearing completion incidents which indicate growth. Results in the thinking, feeling, and responding of boys and girls will enable teachers to recognize those experiences which have been especially meaningful and those which have failed in their purpose. From this evaluation they can plan a better way to guide when the unit is repeated with another group.

When parents and teachers meet together, some of these records should be shared; for in mutual concern for boys and girls will come the finest of Christian fellowship. This will help fathers and mothers to recognize evidences of Christian growth in their families, and to guide and nurture it. When boys and girls are promoted into the next department, their Christian growth during the junior years should be reviewed and evaluated by their parents, the teachers who

have guided them, and those who will guide them as inter-
mediates.

The minister will want to know how the children of the
church are growing. From his own experiences with the
juniors he will contribute to the records. In all his ministry
he will seek and find ways to help both parents and teachers
nurture the growing faith of boys and girls.

Church commissions responsible for Christian education
need reports on how well the juniors are growing. Records
kept by those who work closely with this age group will point
up good growth and indicate needs that are not being met.
Boys and girls in a downtown city church may lack guided
religious experiences in the outdoors and opportunities to
live closely together as Christian friends. Hence the commission on education will give thought to a camping program
for juniors. In a rural church where children have little
fellowship during vacation months and where winter attendance may be irregular, a vacation church school will be
doubly important.

The good growth boys and girls are making should be the
largest part of our record keeping. Never should records
become complaints of our difficulties with pupils or classes.
We do need to think of problems, but only as these point the
way to a more comprehensive program of activities or to the
cultivation of closer Christian friendship with a child and
his family.

For You to Do

Think prayerfully about the juniors whom you are guiding. What evidences are there that they are growing in the
faith and in the Christian fellowship? Begin a record for
each one on file cards or on pages in a notebook.

Your Own Growth as a Christian Teacher

From your own growing in the Christian faith comes the
deep, sincere desire to lead boys and girls in the way that

Jesus lived and taught. From your own growing in Christian love comes the spirit that enables you to guide and help all of them, even the least co-operative. From your growth in teaching skills comes the sure touch, the confidence, the creative guiding of experiences, which make the hours you spend with children rich and rewarding for them and for you. From your constantly growing awareness of God's presence and guidance in your own life comes sensitivity to the outreach of boys and girls toward God.

The conscious search to know God more fully leads to daily devotional practices of prayer and meditation, of guided reading and Bible study. These make teachers ready to sense the deep significance of the units in which they guide juniors. Such teachers have spiritual insights and recognize spiritual needs of boys and girls. Sharing in the worship of the church fellowship keeps them conscious of God's purposes for themselves, for Christian people everywhere, and for the world. Thus from their own experiences they are ready to enrich and lift up to new levels of meaning the experiences of their junior group.

Teachers may grow, too, by constantly reviewing and evaluating their guidance of juniors. Make it a habit to think searchingly about each session as soon as possible after it ends. You will, of course, have some "feeling" about it, that it was unusually good, or very difficult, or just fair. However, a teacher must train himself to examine that feeling and what happened in a session to make it good, or average, or poor.

Were your high hopes for the period realized to any extent? Did the boys and girls make important discoveries? Were they interested in the search because they were doing the discovering? If not, did you hurry their thinking, put words into their mouths, approve responses which were like those you had anticipated, but ignore some thinking that was equally good, but different?

Did the group lose interest somewhere along the way? Try to think at what point this happened. Was it when you were doing most of the thinking and talking? Was it due to outside distraction or to an interruption? Did you pause to reprove a junior or allow yourself to become annoyed by something unimportant? Once the trouble is analyzed, you know what to avoid in the next session.

Did the discussion become sidetracked so that the group never found out what they needed to know? When their thinking angled off from the main line, did some good learning result? It often does. How might you skillfully and tactfully have brought the juniors back to their original search?

Was there enough background laid so that the group seemed ready to plan activities? Were the juniors wholehearted about it, or where they just acquiescing to what you wanted them to do? Did you welcome and respect all their suggestions and help them to evaluate these so that they could select wisely, or did you ignore those which seemed less suitable? Did you reject some ideas for activities because you were afraid to try to guide them?

Most of all you will ask yourself whether this was just another "lesson" to the boys and girls or whether the vital spark of Christian experience was there. Did you recognize and use the right moment for sharing with God the learning and planning of the group? Was there a sense of belonging to God as you asked his blessing upon the worthy ways in which you were seeking to live and work together in harmony with him and his will? If not, how will you plan in the next session to reach out for God's help in the creating and strengthening of attitudes?

A sixth-grade class had been reading about the sufferings of the Hebrew people in Egypt. One of the juniors likened this experience to present-day forced-labor camps, to the years of exile many families have endured. "And think," said the teacher, "how during all those years of hardship and cruelty someone was getting ready to help. It was only a boy and one who was growing up in the palace of Pharaoh. That seemed a very unlikely place from which help would come for the Hebrews. Who knows? Perhaps some boy or girl in our class will feel very deeply the needs of the world. Perhaps one of us will grow up to help rid the world of war, or hunger, or hate."

To her astonishment a mist came into the eyes of one boy who sat silently. Was there already something in his experience which made him sensitive to such great needs of the world?

"O God," she prayed softly, and the boys and girls bowed in sincere reverence, "we know that you have hopes and plans for the world in which all of us may have a part. Help us to be learning about the problems of the world. Help us to care deeply about what is happening to other people. May we be getting ready even now to lead the way toward peace and brotherhood. Amen."